Everyday Problem Solving & Reasoning

Make them a part of every maths lesson

Author & Series Editor: Sarah-Anne Fernandes

Published by Keen Kite Books
An imprint of HarperCollins*Publishers* Ltd
1 London Bridge Street
London
SE1 9GF

Images and Illustrations are © Shutterstock.com and © HarperCollins*Publishers* Ltd

Text and design © 2016 Keen Kite Books, an imprint of HarperCollins*Publishers* Ltd

10 9 8 7 6 5 4 3 2 1

ISBN 9780008184681

British Library Cataloguing in Publication Data
A catalogue record for this publication is available from the British Library.

Author: Sarah-Anne Fernandes
Commissioning Editor: Michelle I'Anson
Series Editor: Sarah-Anne Fernandes
Project Management: Fiona Watson, Sally Rigg
Cover Design: Jez Williams
Internal design and illustrations: QBS Learning
Production: Lyndsey Rogers

Contents

Introduction

If pupils are to develop a deepened understanding of the mathematics curriculum it is important that they are given regular opportunities to reason mathematically and to solve increasingly complex problems. This series has been developed with this in mind. It provides 11 key problem solving and reasoning strategies that you can easily embed into daily mathematics lessons.

The series promotes 'mastering' year group content rather than just accelerating to new mathematical concepts and objectives. This will help pupils to develop greater depth of mathematical learning and understanding of the year group content being learned.

Problem solving and reasoning toolkit

There are 11 different strategies that make up the 'Problem solving and reasoning toolkit'. Each strategy is linked to an icon to allow pupils and teachers to easily identify which strategy they are focusing on:

1. Finding all possibilities
2. Finding rules and describing patterns
3. Logic puzzles
4. Real-life word problems
5. Reasoning: True or false
6. Reasoning: Explain how you know
7. Reasoning: Would you rather?
8. Reasoning: Odd one out
9. Reasoning: Always, sometimes, never true?
10. Reasoning: Convince me – What's the same, What's different?
11. Reasoning: If the answer is X, what is the question?

Problem solving and reasoning pupil target sheet

These 11 strategies are drawn together on the problem solving and reasoning pupil target sheet:

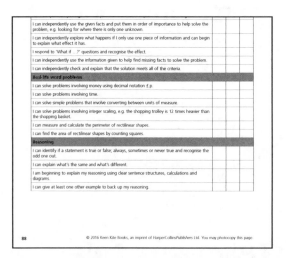

I can independently use the given facts and put them in order of importance to help solve the problem, e.g. looking for where there is only one unknown.			
I can independently explore what happens if I only use one piece of information and can begin to explain what effect it has.			
I respond to 'What if …?' questions and recognise the effect.			
I can independently use the information given to help find missing facts to solve the problem.			
I can independently check and explain that the solution meets all of the criteria.			
Real-life word problems			
I can solve problems involving money using decimal notation £.p.			
I can solve problems involving time.			
I can solve simple problems that involve converting between units of measure.			
I can solve problems involving integer scaling, e.g. the shopping trolley is 12 times heavier than the shopping basket.			
I can measure and calculate the perimeter of rectilinear shapes.			
I can find the area of rectilinear shapes by counting squares.			
Reasoning			
I can identify if a statement is true or false, always, sometimes or never true and recognise the odd one out.			
I can explain what's the same and what's different.			
I am beginning to explain my reasoning using clear sentence structures, calculations and diagrams.			
I can give at least one other example to back up my reasoning.			

88   © 2016 Keen Kite Books, an imprint of HarperCollins*Publishers* Ltd. You may photocopy this page.

The target sheet lists the key skills that pupils need to develop in order to successfully use each of the 11 strategies and can be used as an ongoing assessment tool to track pupils' understanding throughout the year. Although the 11 strategies remain the same across the series, the skills needed to use each strategy get harder throughout each year group, allowing a consistent but progressive approach to be applied to whole-school mathematics problem solving and reasoning.

How to use this book

The book is broken down into two main components:

1. Teaching the strategies and **2.** Topic-by-topic pupil activities.

The first section clearly demonstrates how to teach pupils to use the 11 problem-solving and reasoning strategies. Key features include:

Links to the problem solving and reasoning pupil target sheet.

A list of 'steps to success' for pupils to use when solving problems.

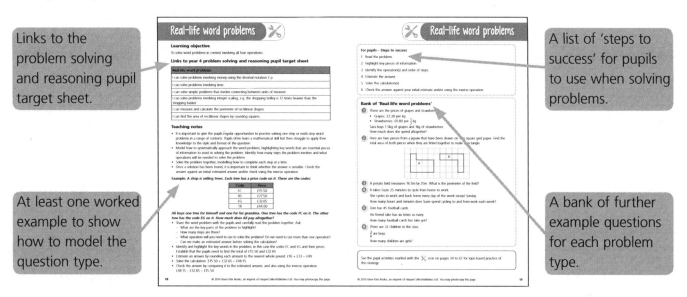

At least one worked example to show how to model the question type.

A bank of further example questions for each problem type.

In the second section, the year group mathematics content domains are addressed through topic-based pupil activities.

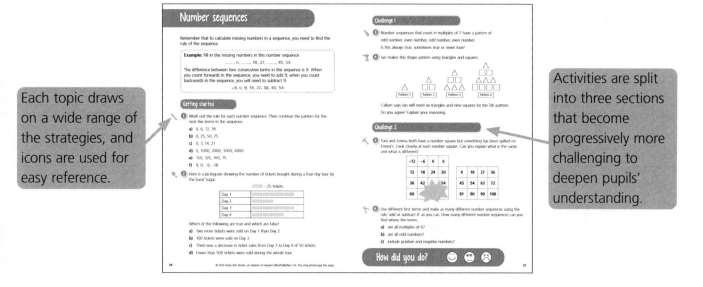

Each topic draws on a wide range of the strategies, and icons are used for easy reference.

Activities are split into three sections that become progressively more challenging to deepen pupils' understanding.

The questions in the book could be used:

- as a warm up at the start of a lesson, for example working in groups to find the 'odd one out' to review learning from the day before
- as a plenary during a lesson, for example solving a logic puzzle where they are having to apply learning from the lesson
- as independent practice to allow pupils to demonstrate understanding of the topics learned
- within guided sessions where teachers and teaching assistants can scaffold pupils' understanding of how to solve the problem.

As the book is also supplied as an editable Word file, questions can be adapted to align to the topics being taught, enabling you to fully embed practice of the 11 strategies across the year. You may also choose to collate individual questions onto cards so pupils are focusing on one type of problem-solving strategy at a time, or to print out a set of 'steps to success' cards to hand out to pupils as a reminder of how to tackle each strategy.

Finding all possibilities

Learning objective

To solve a problem by finding all possible answers.

Links to year 4 problem solving and reasoning pupil target sheet

Finding all possibilities
I respond to and ask questions such as 'What can we try next?' or 'What if …?' to help solve the problem.
I am beginning to develop systematic ways for finding **all** solutions, e.g. looking at one shape at a time or starting with the smallest number.
I am beginning to know the best method to record all possible solutions, e.g. an ordered list.
I can find and prove that I have found all possible answers to a problem.

Teaching notes

- When solving problems of this type, the pupils may begin by using trial and error. However, as they continue to work through the problem, encourage the pupils to follow an organised method so that they are systematic in finding all possible solutions.
- Use practical resources to help the pupils manipulate shapes and numbers in order to find all possible solutions.

Example 1: *Shiv goes out for lunch with his dad. His dad says he can choose three courses and two different toppings for his pizza. List all the different meal choices that Shiv could have.*

> Menu
> *First Course – Starter*
> Garlic bread or Butter bread or Cheese bread
> *Second Course – Main*
> Cheese and tomato pizza with *choice of two toppings:*
> – *Peppers*
> – *Onion*
> – *Mushrooms*
> *Third Course – Pudding*
> Ice-cream or Fruit salad

- Share the problem with the pupils. Ask: Can you explain what you have to do to solve this problem?
- Establish that they need to find all the different meal choices that Shiv could have.
- Remind the pupils of the menu choices that Shiv has to choose from. Then give them a short time to think of different meal choices. Each time they come up with an idea ask:
  - Does the meal choice match the criteria given by Dad?
  - Is this meal choice different to any you previously chose?
- Now look at how the pupils are approaching the problem. Are any pupils approaching the problem in a systematic way or are they just randomly choosing items from the menu?
- Model different ways of ensuring that each possible meal combination is found by selecting the items in a systematic way. Suggest that the pupils could do this by writing an ordered list. Demonstrate how to change only one item at a time.
- Begin by selecting garlic bread for the first course, ice-cream for the third course and choosing the first pizza topping as peppers and adding the other pizza topping options:

✓ **Garlic bread**
Pizza with **peppers** + *onion*
Ice-cream

✓ **Garlic bread**
Pizza with **peppers** + *mushrooms*
Ice-cream

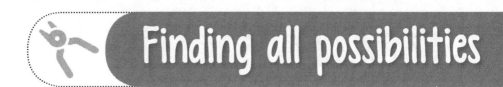

- Now explain that you are going to keep the first and third course the same but change the first pizza topping to onion:

✓ **Garlic bread**
Pizza with **onion** + *mushrooms*
Ice-cream

✓ **Garlic bread**
Pizza with **onion** + *peppers**
Ice-cream

*Establish that this is the same as the choice above [peppers + onion] so cannot be counted as a different meal choice.

- Explain that you are going to still keep the first and third course the same but change the first pizza topping to mushrooms:

✓ **Garlic bread**
Pizza with **mushrooms + *peppers***
Ice-cream

*Establish that this is the same as the choice above [peppers + mushrooms] so cannot be counted as a different meal choice.

✓ **Garlic bread**
Pizza with **mushrooms** + *onion**
Ice-cream

*Establish that this is the same as the choice above [onion + mushrooms] so cannot be counted as a different meal choice.

- Establish that there are three different options when Shiv chooses garlic bread for his starter and ice-cream for pudding.

- Now explain that you are going to change the starter to butter bread but keep the pudding choice as ice-cream. Explain that you will follow the same system as before:

✓ **Butter bread**
Pizza with **peppers** + *onion*
Ice-cream

✓ **Butter bread**
Pizza with **onion** + *mushrooms*
Ice-cream

✓ **Butter bread**
Pizza with **peppers** + *mushrooms*
Ice-cream

✓ **Butter bread**
Pizza with **onion** + *peppers**
Ice-cream

*Establish that this is the same as the choice above [peppers+ onion] so cannot be counted as a different meal choice.

- Ask whether it is necessary to repeat the choices with mushrooms as the first topping. Establish that it is not necessary as 'mushroom + peppers' will be the same 'peppers + mushrooms' and 'mushrooms + onion' is the same as 'onion + mushrooms'. So there are also three different meal options when butter bread is the starter and ice-cream is the pudding. Confirm whether all the meal options have been found for butter bread as the starter and ice-cream as the pudding.

- Encourage the pupils to think about the system and decide what to change next. Establish that next they need to change the starter to cheese bread.

- Give pupils some time to complete and establish that there are three meal options.

✓ **Cheese bread**
Pizza with **peppers** + *onion*
Ice-cream

✓ **Cheese bread**
Pizza with **peppers** + *mushrooms*
Ice-cream

✓ **Cheese bread**
Pizza with **onion** + *mushrooms*
Ice-cream

- Confirm that each starter option has been chosen and ask the pupils what they can now choose differently from the menu. Establish that they can change the pudding choice for each meal from ice-cream to fruit salad.

- Ask: Do you need to choose a different starter again each time?
  - Explain that they will have to choose each of the different starters and pizza toppings again but that this time the pudding will always be fruit salad.

✓ **Garlic bread**
Pizza with **peppers** + *onion*
Fruit salad

✓ **Garlic bread**
Pizza with **peppers** + *mushrooms*
Fruit salad

Finding all possibilities

✓ **Garlic bread**
 Pizza with **onion** + *mushrooms*
 Fruit salad

✓ **Butter bread**
 Pizza with **peppers** + *onion*
 Fruit salad

✓ **Butter bread**
 Pizza with **peppers** + *mushrooms*
 Fruit salad

✓ **Butter bread**
 Pizza with **onion** + *mushrooms*
 Fruit salad

✓ **Cheese bread**
 Pizza with **peppers** + *onion*
 Fruit salad

✓ **Cheese bread**
 Pizza with **peppers** + *mushrooms*
 Fruit salad

✓ **Cheese bread**
 Pizza with **onion** + *mushrooms*
 Fruit salad

- In summary, ask if the pupils have chosen each starter option, each pudding option and two different pizza toppings with each starter or pudding choice. Then establish that there are 18 different possible meal choices for Shiv.

Example 2: *Amy uses these digit cards to make 4-digit whole numbers. How many different numbers can she make?*

$$\boxed{1}\ \boxed{8}\ \boxed{7}\ \boxed{2}$$

- Invite the pupils to explain what they have to do to solve this problem. Establish that they need to find all the different 4-digit numbers that Amy can make using all four of these digit cards each time.
- Encourage the pupils to suggest a good way to begin finding the different numbers so that they use a systematic approach to find all the possible numbers. Establish it would be sensible to start with either the smallest or the largest digit card.
- Begin by placing the largest number card in the 'thousands column' and model how to systematically arrange the numbers moving the hundreds, then the tens and then the ones:

$$\boxed{8}\ \boxed{7}\ \boxed{2}\ \boxed{1} \qquad \boxed{8}\ \boxed{7}\ \boxed{1}\ \boxed{2}$$

$$\boxed{8}\ \boxed{2}\ \boxed{7}\ \boxed{1} \qquad \boxed{8}\ \boxed{2}\ \boxed{1}\ \boxed{7}$$

$$\boxed{8}\ \boxed{1}\ \boxed{2}\ \boxed{7} \qquad \boxed{8}\ \boxed{1}\ \boxed{7}\ \boxed{2}$$

- Ask what digit card should be chosen next in order to be systematic. Establish that it would be sensible to put the second largest number in the thousands column next. Continue in this way until each of the four digit cards has been placed in the thousands column.
- Solution (24 ways): 8721, 8712, 8271, 8217, 8127, 8172; 7821, 7812, 7218, 7281, 7128, 7182; 2871, 2817, 2781, 2718, 2187, 2178; 1278, 1287, 1782, 1728, 1827, 1872

For pupils – Steps to success

1. Read the problem and clearly establish what you need to solve.

2. Begin trying to find one possible solution using the information given, drawing a picture or using equipment if that helps.

3. Try to think of other possible solutions to the problem, using a systematic approach and beginning to create an ordered list.

4. Check each solution given matches the criteria and is not a repeat.

Bank of 'Finding all possibilities' questions

1. The perimeter of a rectangle is 30cm. The width is 3cm, the length is four times greater.

   Calculate the area of this rectangle and then draw all the different rectilinear shapes with the same area on square paper.

2. Pop star Sam is packing for his music tour. When he performs he always wears a pair of trousers, a white shirt, a jacket and a belt.

   List all the different performance outfits he could wear. This is his wardrobe:

Gold trousers Black trousers Purple trousers	White shirt	Silver jacket Stars jacket	Black belt Guitar belt

3. Milly has an L-shape.

   She cuts off two right-angled triangles, as shown:

   Draw the different shapes that Milly can make.

4. Write the number 48 as the product of three numbers.

   How many different ways can you find to do this?

5. Omar says that the number 8976 can be expressed as:

   8 thousands, 9 hundreds, 7 tens, 6 ones

   How many different ways can you find to express the number 8976?

6. Use the digit cards to find as many different ways as possible to make the number sentence correct:

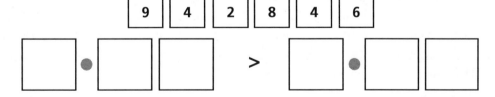

See the pupil activities marked with the icon on pages 34 to 67 for topic-based practice of this strategy.

Finding rules and describing patterns

Learning objective

To solve a problem by finding a rule and describing the pattern.

Links to year 4 problem solving and reasoning pupil target sheet

Finding rules and describing patterns
I can independently describe the rule of a sequence involving numbers or shapes.
I can test if the rule works for other predicted terms in the sequence.
I can independently continue the sequence.
I can independently use the 'found rule' to work out the tenth term in a sequence.

Teaching notes

- When solving problems of this type, pupils need to look carefully to find a rule and begin to describe the pattern.
- It is important to define the meaning of a 'pattern'. Establish that a pattern is an arrangement of numbers, lines or shapes that follow a rule.
- When looking for rules and patterns, give the pupils access to number lines, 100 squares or other concrete resources that may be useful to help them spot the pattern.

Example 1: *Ben wants to find the missing terms in this sequence. Work out the rules and use them to find the missing terms.*

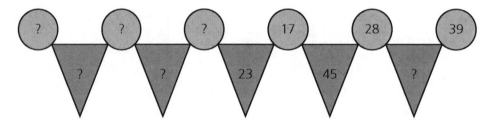

- Share the problem with the pupils. Ask:
  - What is a term?
  - Can we spot a pattern for the circle terms/triangle terms by just looking at the sequence?
  - Do you think the rule for finding the circle terms is different to that for finding the triangle terms?
  - What is the best way to begin finding the rule?
- Establish that a good strategy is to look at the difference between two consecutive terms. Here, the difference between two circle terms is 11 (28 – 17). Ask if the difference of 11 also applies to two other consecutive terms. Prove that the difference between two consecutive circles in the sequence is 11.
- Ask if the circle rule can be applied to the triangles. When the pupils have agreed that it does not work, ask them to begin exploring the pattern for the triangle terms.
  - Is there a relationship between the circle terms and the triangle terms?
  - Are you able to use the strategy of finding the difference between two terms to help find the rule for the triangle terms?

- Help the pupils to see that, to find the triangle terms, they need to either add 22 to find the next term or add together the two circle terms above the triangle.

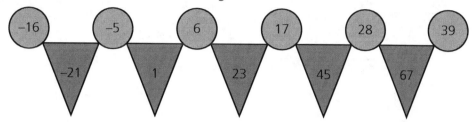

Example 2: *Farmer Jon is making vegetable patches to plant his new crop. He uses logs to make a vegetable patch like this:*

He now makes a second vegetable patch next to it, like this:

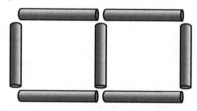

He continues making vegetable patches. Work out the number pattern rule. Use this to calculate how many logs are needed to make 10 vegetable patches.

- Share the problem with the pupils. Ask: What are you trying to find out?
- Establish that they must try to find a pattern so that they can calculate how many logs are needed to make 10 vegetable patches without having to make or draw them. Explain that, once they establish the pattern, they could use this to work out how many logs would be needed to make 15 vegetable patches, 50 vegetable patches and so on.
- Ask:
  - Can you spot a pattern from looking at the first two vegetable patches?
  - What is a term?
  - How many logs are needed for one vegetable patch?
  - How many logs are needed for two vegetable patches?
  - What may be a good way of drawing this information together?
- Model putting the information into a table like the one shown below. Ask:
  - Are you beginning to see a pattern? Can you explain it?
  - How many logs do you think are needed for four vegetable patches? How can you prove whether your prediction is correct?

Number of vegetable patches	Number of logs
1	4
2	7
3	10
4	?

Finding rules and describing patterns

- Agree that the pattern seems to increase by three each time from the starting point of four logs.
- Therefore, predict that 13 logs will be needed to build four vegetable patches.
- In order to convince themselves that their prediction is correct, suggest that the pupils make or draw four vegetable patches.

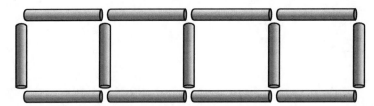

- Establish that the prediction is correct and that the pattern works.
- Now encourage the pupils to use this pattern to find the number of logs needed for up to 10 vegetable patches and to complete their tables.

Number of vegetable patches	Number of logs
1	4
2	7
3	10
4	13
5	16
6	19
7	22
8	25
9	28
10	31

For pupils – Steps to success

1. Look carefully at the numbers or shapes.

2. Begin to look for a pattern and start exploring what the rule could be.

3. Test the rule with different terms to check it works.

4. Apply the rule to generate unknown terms.

Bank of 'Finding rules and describing patterns' questions

1 Here is part of a number sequence. The numbers increase by the same amount each time.

750   755   760   765   770

The sequence continues. Circle all the numbers below that would appear in the sequence.

840   905   898   1000   2051

2 Use a circle like the one shown below to explore patterns from the multiplication facts by plotting the value of the ones digit. For example, for the three times table, plot the underlined digits shown here on the wheel: <u>3</u>, <u>6</u>, <u>9</u>, 1<u>2</u>, 1<u>5</u>, 1<u>8</u>, 2<u>1</u>, 2<u>4</u>, 2<u>7</u>, 3<u>0</u>, 3<u>3</u>, 3<u>6</u>

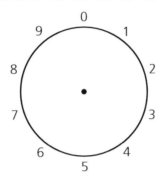

What patterns and rules do you notice for different times tables?

3 Here is part of a number square. The shaded numbers are part of a sequence. Explain the rule for the sequence.

113	114	115	116
123	124	125	126
133	134	135	136
143	144	145	146

4 Copy and complete this number pattern.

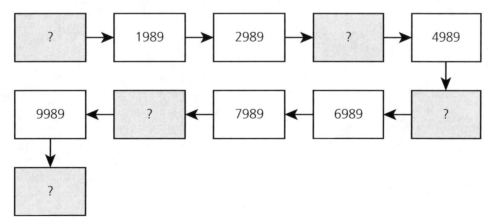

See the pupil activities marked with the icon on pages 34 to 67 for topic-based practice of this strategy.

Learning objective

To solve logic puzzles.

Links to year 4 problem solving and reasoning pupil target sheet

Logic puzzles
I can independently recognise some patterns and relationships in the information given.
I can independently use the given facts and put them in order of importance to help solve the problem, e.g. looking for where there is only one unknown.
I can independently explore what happens if I only use one piece of information and can begin to explain what effect it has.
I can respond to 'What if …?' questions and recognise the effect.
I can independently use the information given to help find missing facts to solve the problem.
I can independently check and explain that the solution meets all of the criteria.

Teaching notes

- Pupils may begin by using trial and error to solve problems of this type. Explain that a good place to start is to look for where there is only one unknown.
- Model how to identify the key information and the aim of the problem.
- Model how to work systematically using the clues provided.
- Pupils will need to use their knowledge of all four operations to solve logic puzzles.

Example 1: *Use your multiplication and division facts to work out the value of each symbol.*

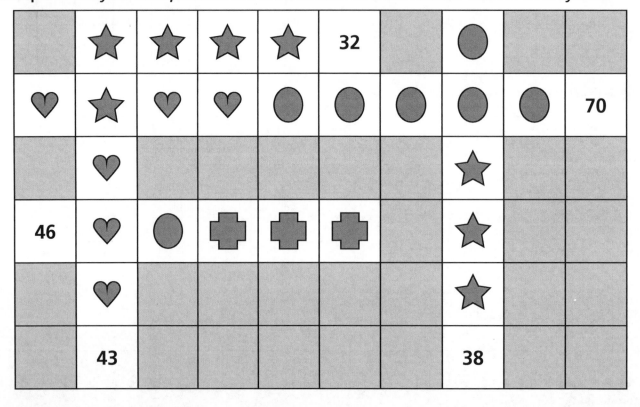

© 2016 Keen Kite Books, an imprint of HarperCollins*Publishers* Ltd. You may photocopy this page.

- Share the problem with the pupils, asking what symbols they need to find the value of. Establish that they need to find the value of the following four symbols:

- Elicit from the pupils what the really important pieces of information in the puzzle are. Emphasise that the totals of each row or column are critical pieces of information and that without this they could not solve the problem. Model what each total on the puzzle refers to and then ask the pupils to join in.
  - 32 is the total of the first row and is made up of four stars.
  - 70 is the total of the second row and is made up of five circles, three hearts and one star.
  - 46 is the total of the third row and is made up of one heart, one circle and three crosses.
  - 43 is the total of the first column and is made up of two stars and three hearts.
  - 38 is the total of the second column and is made up of two circles and three stars.
- Ask the pupils if they think they have enough information to solve the puzzle and where the best place to start is. Establish that the best place to start is on the first row where four circles are equal to 32 because here there is only one unknown symbol. This means that they can divide the total (32) by the number of stars to work out the value of one star: 32 ÷ 4 = 8, so 8 is the value of one star.
- Encourage the pupils to decide which column or row to tackle next and to explain why. Discuss that it is best to do either the first column (two stars + three hearts) or the second column (two circles + three stars) next. Explain that, because we now know the value of the star, both these columns only have one unknown to work out.
- Model how to find the value of the heart in the first column. Subtract 16 (i.e. two stars) from the total of the column: 43 – 16 = 27, and then divide 27 by the total number of hearts in the column: 27 ÷ 3 = 9, so 9 is the value of one heart.
- Ask which column or row they should do next and why. Determine that either the second row or the second column could be done next to find the value of the circle because both these now only contain one unknown. However, suggest that it would be more time efficient and less complex to find the value of the circle using the second column because it only contains stars and circles.
- Model how to calculate the value of the circle. Subtract 24 (i.e. three stars) from the total of the column: 38 – 24 = 14, and then divide 14 by the total number of circles in the column: 14 ÷ 2 = 7, so 7 is the value of one circle.
- Establish that the final puzzle is to find the value of the cross symbol and that the values of all the other symbols in the third row are now known. Model how to find the value of the cross by subtracting the value of the heart (9) and the value of the circle (7) from the total of the row: 46 – 9 – 7 = 30, then divide 30 by the number of crosses that are in the row: 30 ÷ 3 = 10, so 10 is the value of one cross.
- Remind the pupils to check the puzzle by writing the value of each symbol into the puzzle to ensure that the total of each row/column correctly adds up.

Logic puzzles

Example 2: *In a fruit bowl, $\frac{1}{6}$ of the fruit are apples and $\frac{1}{3}$ of the fruit are pears. There are also three bananas, five oranges and one mango. How many apples are in the bowl? How many pieces of fruit are there altogether?*

- Share the problem with the pupils. Ask them to explain what they have to do to solve this problem. Establish that they need to find out how many apples there are and how many pieces of fruit there are altogether.
- Ask:
  - What are the key pieces of information in the problem?
  - How many sixths and thirds do you need to make a whole?
  - How many pieces of fruit are known? What fraction is this of all the fruit? How do you know that?
- Model how to use a fraction bar to help solve the problem. Insert the information given.

1 whole = pieces of fruit in the bowl in total		
$\frac{1}{6}$ of the fruit are apples	$\frac{1}{3}$ of the fruit are pears	so the rest of the fruit must total one-half

- Help the pupils realise that, from the information given in the problem, they can tell that the 'rest of the fruit' is equal to three bananas + five oranges + one mango which equals nine pieces of fruit. Therefore $\frac{1}{2}$ = nine pieces.
- Demonstrate how to use this information to complete the fraction bar.

1 whole = pieces of fruit in the bowl in total		
$\frac{1}{6}$ of the fruit are apples	$\frac{1}{3}$ of the fruit are pears	the rest of the fruit must total one-half
3 apples	6 pears	3 bananas + 5 oranges + 1 mango = 9 pieces of fruit

For pupils – Steps to success

1. Read the problem and clearly establish what you need to solve.

2. Identify the most useful information.

3. Begin where there is only one unknown.

4. Use one piece of information at a time to systematically solve the problem.

Bank of 'Logic puzzles' questions

1 Complete this diagram so that the three numbers in each line add up to 150

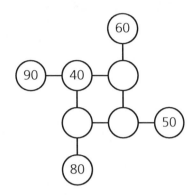

2 Work out the value of each symbol and calculate the missing totals.

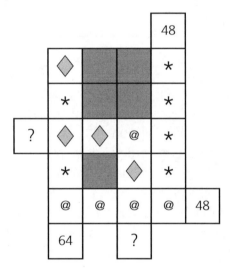

3 In this diagram, the number in each box is the sum of the numbers in the two boxes below it.

Work out the value of the missing numbers.

		?		
	?	?	
$\frac{6}{8}$	?	$\frac{7}{8}$
?	$\frac{2}{8}$	$\frac{3}{8}$	?

4 Sue and Amy are playing 'guess my number'. Sue says: 'I subtract 1145 from my number to get 4370.' Amy says: 'My number is 1065 more than Sue's number.'

Work out what each of their numbers is.

See the pupil activities marked with the icon on pages 34 to 67 for topic-based practice of this strategy.

Learning objective

To solve word problems in context involving all four operations.

Links to year 4 problem solving and reasoning pupil target sheet

Real-life word problems
I can solve problems involving money using the decimal notation £.p.
I can solve problems involving time.
I can solve simple problems that involve converting between units of measure.
I can solve problems involving integer scaling, e.g. the shopping trolley is 12 times heavier than the shopping basket.
I can measure and calculate the perimeter of rectilinear shapes.
I can find the area of rectilinear shapes by counting squares.

Teaching notes

- It is important to give the pupils regular opportunities to practise solving one-step or multi-step word problems in a range of contexts. Pupils often learn a mathematical skill but then struggle to apply their knowledge to the style and format of the question.
- Model how to systematically approach the word problem, highlighting key words that are essential pieces of information to assist in solving the problem. Identify how many steps the problem involves and what operations will be needed to solve the problem.
- Solve the problem together, modelling how to complete each step at a time.
- Once a solution has been found, it is important to think whether the answer is sensible. Check the answer against an initial estimated answer and/or check using the inverse operation.

Example: _A shop is selling trees. Each tree has a price code on it. These are the codes:_

Code	Price
FC	£15.50
BS	£27.50
EG	£32.65
TR	£44.00

Ali buys one tree for himself and one for his grandma. One tree has the code FC on it. The other tree has the code EG on it. How much does Ali pay altogether?

- Share the word problem with the pupils and carefully read the problem together. Ask:
  - What are the key parts of the problem to highlight?
  - How many steps are there?
  - What operation will you need to use to solve the problem? Do we need to use more than one operation?
  - Can we make an estimated answer before solving the calculation?
- Identify and highlight the key words in the problem, in this case the codes FC and EG and their prices. Establish that the pupils need to find the total of £15.50 and £32.65
- Estimate an answer by rounding each amount to the nearest whole pound: £16 + £33 = £49
- Solve the calculation: £15.50 + £32.65 = £48.15
- Check the answer by comparing it to the estimated answer, and also using the inverse operation £48.15 − £32.65 = £15.50

Real-life word problems

For pupils – Steps to success

1. Read the problem.

2. Highlight key pieces of information.

3. Identify the operation(s) and order of steps.

4. Estimate the answer.

5. Solve the calculation(s).

6. Check the answer against your initial estimate and/or using the inverse operation.

Bank of 'Real-life word problems'

1 These are the prices of grapes and strawberries:

- Grapes: £2.20 per kg
- Strawberries: £0.80 per $\frac{1}{2}$ kg

Sara buys 1.5kg of grapes and 1kg of strawberries.
How much does she spend altogether?

2 Here are two pieces from a jigsaw that have been drawn on 1cm square grid paper. Find the total area of both pieces when they are fitted together to make a rectangle.

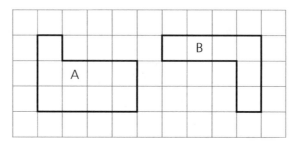

3 A potato field measures 16.5m by 25m. What is the perimeter of the field?

4 It takes Suzie 25 minutes to cycle from home to work.

She cycles to work and back home every day of the week except Sunday.

How many hours and minutes does Suzie spend cycling to and from work each week?

5 Tom has 45 football cards.

His friend Jake has six times as many.

How many football cards has Jake got?

6 There are 32 children in the class.

$\frac{3}{8}$ are boys.

How many children are girls?

See the pupil activities marked with the icon on pages 34 to 67 for topic-based practice of this strategy.

Reasoning: True or false

Learning objective

To identify whether a statement is true or false and explain why.

Links to year 4 problem solving and reasoning pupil target sheet

Reasoning
I can identify if a statement is true or false.
I am beginning to explain my reasoning using clear sentence structures, calculations and diagrams.
I can give at least one other example to back up my reasoning.

Teaching notes

- The strategy 'true or false' requires pupils to prove a statement is correct or incorrect by using calculations and mathematical diagrams to support their reasoning.
- True or false questions can be applied to any curriculum content area and can be used as a simple warm-up reasoning activity or made more complex to encourage good mathematical debate.

Example: *Look at each division fact and decide if it is true or false.*

$9 \div 100 = 0.9$ $\qquad$ $56 \div 10 = 5.6$ $\qquad$ $68 \div 100 = 680$ $\qquad$ $7 \div 10 = 0.07$

- Share the problem with the pupils. Ask: Is it possible for all the statements to be true? Is it possible for all the statements to be false?
- Discuss that either is feasible but we cannot make a decision without looking carefully at each statement in turn.
- Discuss that, in order to decide if each statement is true or false, it would be useful to think about what we know about dividing by 10 and 100.
  - What happens to the size of the number when we divide it?
  - What happens to the place value of the digits when we divide by 10? How do the digits move?
  - What happens to the place value of the digits when we divide by 100? How do the digits move?
- Point out that when we divide by 10 and 100 the number either gets 10 times smaller or 100 times smaller. Using a place value chart, demonstrate how the digits move one place to the right when dividing by 10 and two places to the right when dividing by 100.

	Thousands	Hundreds	Tens	Ones	·	Tenths	Hundredths
				9	·		
÷10				0	·	9	
÷100				0	·	0	9
			5	6	·		
÷10				5	·	6	
÷100				0	·	5	6

- Encourage the pupils to not just say whether a statement is true or false but to explain why.
- Take each statement in turn and model how to answer it.
  - $9 \div 100 = 0.9$
    This statement is false because the place value of the digit 9 needs to move two places to the right, so the correct answer is 0.09
  - $56 \div 10 = 5.6$
    This statement is true because the place value of each digit moves one place to the right when dividing by 10

- 68 ÷ 100 = 680

  This statement is false because when you divide the number gets smaller not larger. The correct answer is 0.68

- 7 ÷ 10 = 0.07

  This statement is false because, when you divide by 10, the place value of each digit moves one place to the right, so the correct answer is 0.7

For pupils – Steps to success

1. Read the statements and think about the context of the statements.
2. Establish any known facts about the context of the statements.
3. Take each statement in turn and decide whether it is true or false.
4. Give an explanation to prove and explain your thinking.

Bank of 'True or false' questions

1 Decide if each statement is true or false:

a) 1.11 = 1.21   **b)** 1.24 < 1.39   **c)** 1.49 > 1.08   **d)** 1.98 < 1.70

2 Amelie labels these triangles. Work out which triangles have been labelled correctly and rename the triangles that are incorrectly labelled.

a)   **b)**   **c)**   **d)**

Scalene triangle   Equilateral triangle   Isosceles triangle   Right-angled triangle

3 Henry has completed four calculations. Check which are correct and which are incorrect. For the calculations that are incorrect, work out the correct answer.

a) $\frac{3}{6} + \frac{4}{6} = 1\frac{1}{6}$ **b)** $\frac{8}{10} - \frac{4}{10} = \frac{12}{10}$ **c)** $\frac{4}{5} + \frac{2}{5} = 1$ **d)** $\frac{3}{4} - \frac{2}{4} = \frac{1}{4}$

4 Ryan uses this fraction wall to make the following statements. Decide which are true and which are false.

a) $\frac{2}{5} = \frac{4}{10}$ **b)** $\frac{1}{12} = \frac{1}{6}$

c) $\frac{2}{8} = \frac{1}{4}$ **d)** $\frac{3}{12} = \frac{1}{5}$

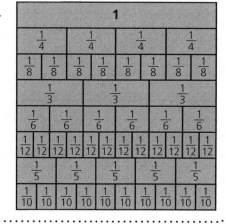

5 Kim says that all these fractions are equivalent to a half.

$$\frac{5}{10} \qquad \frac{3}{8} \qquad \frac{2}{4} \qquad \frac{7}{12} \qquad \frac{15}{20}$$

Is this true or false? Explain your reasoning.

See the pupil activities marked with the icon on pages 34 to 67 for topic-based practice of this strategy.

Reasoning: Explain how you know

Learning objective

To give an explanation using correct mathematical vocabulary, calculations and diagrams.

Links to year 4 problem solving and reasoning pupil target sheet

Reasoning
I am beginning to explain my reasoning using clear sentence structures, calculations and diagrams.
I can give at least one other example to back up my reasoning.

Teaching notes

- This strategy requires the pupils to explain their mathematical thinking clearly and concisely.
- Encourage the pupils to use correct mathematical language, diagrams and calculations to 'explain how they know'.
- It may be helpful to have a bank of sentence starters for pupils to use, such as:
  - *I think this because …*
  - *I agree with … because I know …*
  - *This can't work because …*
  - *When I calculated … I noticed that … so this can/cannot be correct.*
  - *… is correct/incorrect because I know that …*

Example: *Megan says a quadrilateral always has four right angles. Do you agree – yes or no? Explain how you know.*

- Share the problem with the pupils. Ask what they know about four-sided 2-D shapes.
- Can the pupils tell you whether all four-sided shapes are squares? Establish that other 2-D shapes also have four sides.
- Share different responses to the question:

Do you agree? Yes or (No) Explain how you know. *Because the answer is no.*	Do you agree? Yes or (No) Explain how you know. *A rhombus is a quadrilateral and it has no right angles.*	Do you agree? Yes or (No) Explain how you know. *I know this is not true because only some quadrilaterals have four right angles. A square and a rectangle have four right angles but a parallelogram and a rhombus do not have any right angles.*

- Read each of the different responses and together agree which is the best explanation, which is acceptable and which is not acceptable.
- Agree that the third response is the best response, the first is unacceptable and the second is acceptable but lacks detail.
- Challenge the pupils to say how the best response could be further improved. Establish that diagrams could be used to support the explanation. For example:

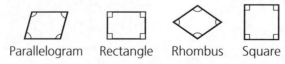

Parallelogram   Rectangle   Rhombus   Square

For pupils – Steps to success

1. Read the question.

2. Solve the problem by using known facts or solving the calculation.

3. Use a sentence starter and complete the explanation using mathematical vocabulary, diagrams and calculations.

Bank of 'Explain how you know' questions

1. Daniel says two-thirds of the diagram has been shaded.

   Do you agree? Explain how you know.

   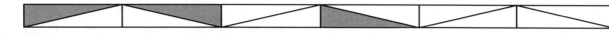

2. Katja says the measurement on this scale shows more than 1000g but less than 1500g.

   Do you agree? Explain how you know.

3. TJ and Eddie are counting in multiples of 1000. TJ says 5050 will appear in the counting sequence. Eddie says this is impossible.

   Who do you agree with? Explain how you know.

4. Su wants to make 18 cookies but she only has a recipe to make 6 cookies.

   Raj says she needs to use four times as much of all the ingredients in the recipe.

   Do you agree? Explain how you know.

5. Amy says it is impossible to draw a square with an area of 18cm^2 where the side is a whole number of centimetres long. Ben says she is correct.

   Do you agree? Explain your reasoning.

See the pupil activities marked with the icon on pages 34 to 67 for topic-based practice of this strategy.

Reasoning: Would you rather?

Learning objective

To choose between two options and explain the reasons for the choice.

Links to year 4 problem solving and reasoning pupil target sheet

Reasoning
I am beginning to explain my reasoning using clear sentence structures, calculations and diagrams.
I can give at least one other example to back up my reasoning.

Teaching notes

- This strategy requires the pupils to reason and explain why they would choose one option over another.
- Pupils will need to solve the calculation for each option given and then justify which one they would choose giving a clear explanation. They can support their explanations with calculations and diagrams.
- Setting the 'would you rather?' problem in an engaging context such as 'Would you rather have 79 minutes of playtime or 3600 seconds of playtime?' can be motivating for pupils.

Example: *Would you rather have $\frac{5}{6}$ of £42 or $\frac{6}{8}$ of £40?*

- Share the problem with the pupils. Without working out the calculation, ask the pupils which fractional amount they think they would prefer and why.
- Discuss that, in order to choose what they would rather have, they need to compare each amount fairly by calculating the fractional amount of each quantity.
- Together work out what calculations should be completed and what operations the pupils will use.
- Establish that there are two different amounts of money and two different fractions. In order to choose the preferred amount, the pupils need to find $\frac{5}{6}$ of £42 and $\frac{6}{8}$ of £40.

  Calculate $\frac{5}{6}$ of £42: $\frac{1}{6}$ of £42 = 42 ÷ 6 = £7, so $\frac{5}{6}$ of £42 = £7 × 5 = £35

  Calculate $\frac{6}{8}$ of £40: $\frac{1}{8}$ of £40 = 40 ÷ 8 = £5, so $\frac{6}{8}$ of £40 = £5 × 6 = £30

  So, assuming you want the larger amount of money, it would be better to have $\frac{5}{6}$ of £42

- Model how pupils could write their final reasoning strategy: 'I would rather have $\frac{5}{6}$ of £42 because I would get £5 more than if I chose $\frac{6}{8}$ of £40.'

Reasoning: Would you rather?

For pupils – Steps to success

1. Read the 'Would you rather?' statement.

2. Calculate or convert both options given in the statement so you can compare fairly.

3. Compare both options.

4. Choose your preferred option.

5. Write an explanation to show your preference using calculations and/or diagrams to support your reasoning.

Bank of 'Would you rather?' questions

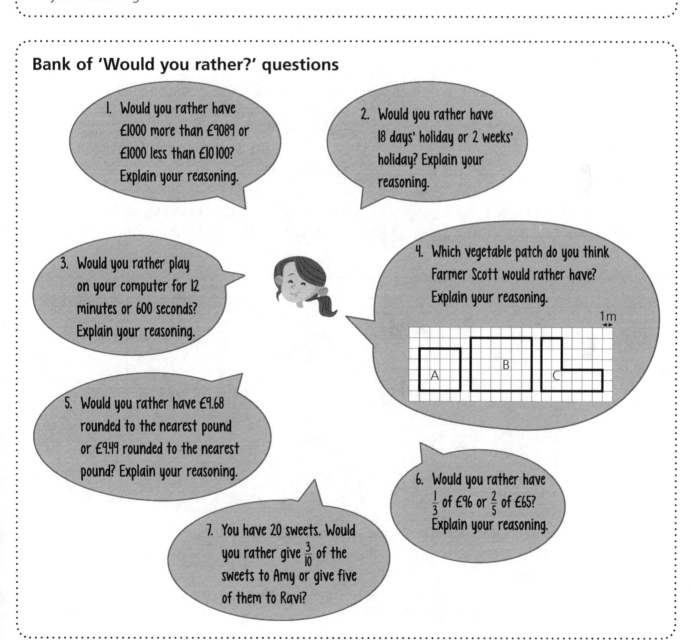

1. Would you rather have £1000 more than £9089 or £1000 less than £10 100? Explain your reasoning.

2. Would you rather have 18 days' holiday or 2 weeks' holiday? Explain your reasoning.

3. Would you rather play on your computer for 12 minutes or 600 seconds? Explain your reasoning.

4. Which vegetable patch do you think Farmer Scott would rather have? Explain your reasoning.

5. Would you rather have £9.68 rounded to the nearest pound or £9.49 rounded to the nearest pound? Explain your reasoning.

6. Would you rather have $\frac{1}{3}$ of £96 or $\frac{2}{5}$ of £65? Explain your reasoning.

7. You have 20 sweets. Would you rather give $\frac{3}{10}$ of the sweets to Amy or give five of them to Ravi?

See the pupil activities marked with the ✂ icon on pages 34 to 67 for topic-based practice of this strategy.

Reasoning: Odd one out

Learning objective

To reason and prove that an item in a set is the odd one out.

Links to year 4 problem solving and reasoning pupil target sheet

Reasoning
I can recognise the odd one out.
I am beginning to explain my reasoning using clear sentence structures, calculations and diagrams.
I can give at least one other example to back up my reasoning.

Teaching notes

- This strategy requires deeper reasoning than some of the other reasoning strategies outlined in this resource. This is because pupils must first look for common features across all items in the set before they can begin to prove why an item in the set is the odd one out. For example: All but one shape in the set of items has four sides.
- Once pupils have formed a generalisation, they can then begin to prove why each item is or is not the odd one out.
- Sometimes pupils struggle to spot a generality between the different items of the set. If this is the case, it can be useful to draw on the reasoning strategy: 'What's the same? What's different?' to help them think of generalisations.

Example: *Look at these numbers. Which is the odd one out?*

125	250	175
	100	
	110	150

- Share the problem with the pupils. Ask:
  - What can you initially spot from looking at each item in the set of numbers?
  - Are all the numbers 3-digit numbers?
  - Do they all end in a 0 or 5?
  - Do all the numbers that end in a 0 also have a value in the tens column?
  - Why might 100 be the odd one out? Why might 250 be the odd one out?
- The pupils may justify that 100 is the odd one out because it is the only number in the set that has a value of zero in the tens column. This answer is valid and perfectly acceptable.
- However, try to probe for another number in the set that is the odd one out. Ask:
  - Are they all multiples of 100? If not, why not?
  - Is there a counting pattern when you put the numbers in order?
  - Do the numbers match to another multiple?
- Establish that all the numbers in the set except 110 are multiples of 25

Reasoning: Odd one out

For pupils – Steps to success

1. Look carefully at each item in the set.

2. Ask what is the same and what is different about the items in the set.

3. Look for patterns and begin to form generalisations to explain why one item may be the odd one out.

Bank of 'Odd one out' questions

1 Which is the odd one out?

a) **b)** **c)** **d)**

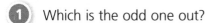

2 Which is the odd one out?

a) 0.4   **b)** $\frac{4}{10}$ **c)**   **d)** four-tenths

3 When rounding to the nearest whole number, which is the odd one out?

a) 7.89   **b)** 4.56   **c)** 8.24   **d)** 9.99   **e)** 1.87

4 Which is the odd one out?

a) $\frac{2}{3}$ of 15   **b)** $\frac{4}{10}$ of 100   **c)** $\frac{1}{4}$ of 40   **d)** $\frac{1}{2}$ of 20

5 Which is the odd one out?

a) **b)** **c)** **d)**

6 Which is the odd one out?

a) 67.45   **b)** 76.87   **c)** 9.00   **d)** 2.32   **e)** 6.53

See the pupil activities marked with the icon on pages 34 to 67 for topic-based practice of this strategy.

Reasoning: Always, sometimes, never true?

Learning objective

To prove if a statement is always, sometimes or never true.

Links to year 4 problem solving and reasoning pupil target sheet

Reasoning
I can identify if a statement is always, sometimes or never true.
I am beginning to explain my reasoning using clear sentence structures, calculations and diagrams.
I can give at least one other example to back up my reasoning.

Teaching notes

- Take a statement that can be always true, sometimes true or never true. Display and discuss it with the pupils.
- Model how to reason effectively by asking questions to support the pupils' thinking.
- Once the pupils have agreed if the statement is always true, sometimes true or never true, model how to make a conjecture and back it up with at least one mathematical example.

Example: *A polygon has straight sides and all the sides are of equal length.*

- Share the statement with the pupils. Ask:
  - What shapes do we know that have straight sides?
  - Are these shapes called polygons?
  - Does our conclusion that straight-sided shapes are called polygons match some of the statement?
  - Do polygons have equal sides?
  - What type of polygon has equal sides?
  - Does the statement use the term 'regular'?
- Highlight that, because the statement does not use 'regular', we cannot say the statement is always true but we can say that it is sometimes true.
- Model how to make a final reasoning statement: 'I believe this statement is sometimes true because a polygon does have straight sides, for example a square, but a polygon does not always have equal length sides because there are irregular polygons, for example a rectangle.'

Regular polygon   Irregular polygon

Reasoning: Always, sometimes, never true?

For pupils – Steps to success

1. Look at the statement.

2. Identify key mathematical vocabulary in the statement.

3. Think of examples to prove or disprove the statement.

4. Explain in a sentence why you think the statement is either always true, sometimes true or never true.

Bank of 'Always, sometimes, never true?' questions

1. When you are rounding decimals with one decimal place to the nearest whole number, the value of the tenths helps to decide whether to round up or round down.

2. 10 metres is equivalent to 10 centimetres.

3. Clocks show am or pm.

4. Two right angles add up to the size of an acute angle.

5. The perimeter is the total distance around a shape.

6. These two fractions of the same quantity are never equivalent: $\frac{1}{5}$ and $\frac{2}{3}$

See the pupil activities marked with the icon on pages 34 to 67 for topic-based practice of this strategy.

Learning objective

To identify what is the same and what is different and explain why.

Links to year 4 problem solving and reasoning pupil target sheet

Reasoning
I can explain what's the same and what's different.
I am beginning to explain my reasoning using clear sentence structures, calculations and diagrams.
I can give at least one other example to back up my reasoning.

Teaching notes

- This strategy encourages pupils to look for connections across the items in the set.
- Begin by asking the pupils to compare and contrast two things; as they become more confident with their reasoning skills, you can extend the set to include more than two items.
- Steer the pupils towards mathematical conjectures rather than sweeping superficial statements such as 'they are the same because they are all shapes'.

Example: *What is the same and what is different about these shapes?*

  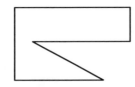 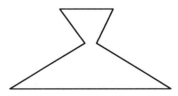

- Share the problem with the pupils.
- First encourage the pupils to think about what is the same about these shapes. Establish that they are all 2-D shapes. They are all polygons as they have straight sides. They all have six sides and so they are all hexagons.
- Next get the pupils to think about what is different about these shapes. Establish that only one is a regular polygon while the others are irregular polygons. Also, establish that only one of these polygons has four right angles.
- Model writing up the pupils' findings in a table.

Same	Different
2-D shapes	Regular or irregular
Polygons	Only one of the hexagons has right angles
Six sides and vertices	
Hexagons	

Reasoning: Convince me – What's the same? What's different?

For pupils – Steps to success

1. Look at each item in the set.

2. Think about what is the same across all items in the set.

3. Think about what is different about the items in the set.

4. Ensure the reasons are mathematical.

Bank of 'Convince me – What's the same? What's different?' questions

1 What is the same and what is different about this set of numbers?

- 5 thousands, 3 hundreds, 1 ten, 5 ones
- 53 hundreds, 1 ten, 5 ones
- 5 thousands, 3 hundreds, 15 ones

2 What is the same and what is different?

$\frac{2}{5}$ 0.4

3 What is the same and what is different about these shapes?

Parallelogram   Rectangle   Rhombus   Square

4 What is the same and what is different about these times?

1 week   7 days   168 hours

5 Look at these charts. What is the same, what is different?

Blackbird	IIII
Sparrow	II
Robin	IIII I
Blue tit	II
Other	IIII III

Number of different types of birds

Number of birds	
Blackbird	🐦 🐦
Sparrow	🐦
Robin	🐦 🐦 🐦
Blue tit	🐦
Other	🐦 🐦 🐦 🐦
Key: 🐦 represents 2 birds	

Type of bird	Number of birds
Blackbird	4
Sparrow	2
Robin	6
Blue tit	2
Other	8

See the pupil activities marked with the icon on pages 34 to 67 for topic-based practice of this strategy.

Learning objective

To come up with as many different questions as possible that could have given a particular answer.

Links to year 4 problem solving and reasoning pupil target sheet

Reasoning
I am beginning to explain my reasoning using clear sentence structures, calculations and diagrams.
I can give at least one other example to back up my reasoning.

Teaching notes

- This strategy encourages pupils to understand that there can be more than one answer to a problem.
- Prompt the pupils to look for patterns to help them generate more possible questions. For example, if the answer is 6000, the question could be:
  - 5000 + 1000
  - 4000 + 2000
  - 3000 + 3000
  - 2000 + 4000*
  - 1000 + 5000*

  *Ask the pupils to consider if these questions are different to the questions above.
- Encourage the pupils to think across a range of mathematical ideas so that their answers are not too repetitive or always using the same operation.

Example: *If the answer is $\frac{4}{10}$, what is the question?*

- Show the pupils the following possible questions that could match the answer $\frac{4}{10}$
- Model how to use a mind map and explicitly discuss with the pupils how the questions draw on different year 4 curriculum content areas.

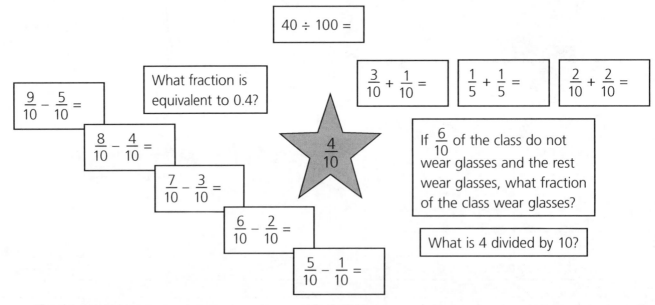

For pupils – Steps to success

1. Write the answer in the centre of the page.

2. Find as many different questions as possible to match the answer given:
   - Look for patterns to generate different questions.
   - Think about different areas of mathematics to find a range of questions.

Bank of 'If the answer is X, what is the question?' questions

1 The answer to the calculation is 2000, so what could the question be? For example: If a school has 75% boys and there are 1500 boys, how many pupils are there in the school altogether?

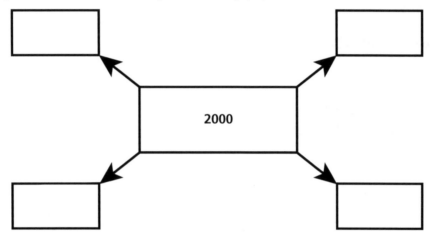

2 If the answer is £10.50, what could the question be?

3 The answer is 6500m. What could the question be?

4 If the answer is 18, what could the question be?

5 If the answer is twenty to six in the evening, what could the question be?

6 If the answer is $\frac{1}{3}$, what is the question?

7 If the answer is five-tenths, what is the question?

8 If the answer is 2kg, what is the question?

See the pupil activities marked with the icon on pages 34 to 67 for topic-based practice of this strategy.

Number sequences

Remember that to calculate missing numbers in a sequence, you need to find the rule of the sequence.

Example: Fill in the missing numbers in this number sequence.

____, 0, ____, 18, 27, ____, 45, 54

The difference between two consecutive terms in the sequence is 9. When you count forwards in the sequence, you need to add 9; when you count backwards in the sequence, you will need to subtract 9.

−9, 0, **9**, 18, 27, **36**, 45, 54

Getting started

1. Work out the rule for each number sequence. Then continue the pattern for the next five terms in the sequence.

   a) 0, 6, 12, 18

   b) 0, 25, 50, 75

   c) 0, 7, 14, 21

   d) 0, 1000, 2000, 3000, 4000

   e) 150, 125, 100, 75

   f) 9, 0, −9, −18

2. Here is a pictogram showing the number of tickets bought during a four-day tour by the band Sugar.

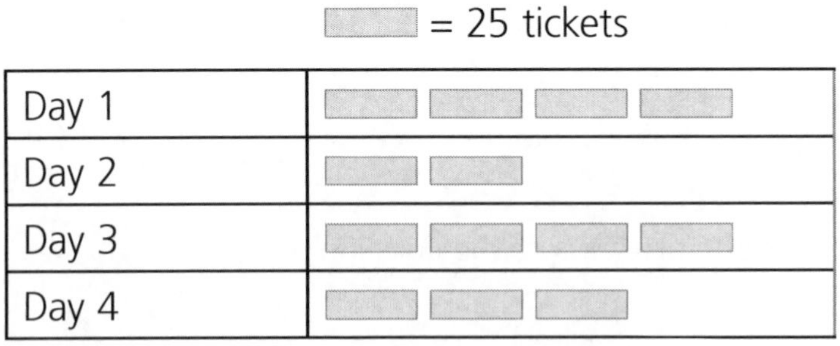

   ▭ = 25 tickets

Day 1	▭ ▭ ▭ ▭
Day 2	▭ ▭
Day 3	▭ ▭ ▭ ▭
Day 4	▭ ▭ ▭

   Which of the following are true and which are false?

   a) Two more tickets were sold on Day 1 than Day 2.

   b) 100 tickets were sold on Day 3.

   c) There was a decrease in ticket sales from Day 3 to Day 4 of 50 tickets.

   d) Fewer than 500 tickets were sold during the whole tour.

Challenge 1

 3 Number sequences that count in multiples of 7 have a pattern of:

odd number, even number, odd number, even number.

Is this always true, sometimes true or never true?

 4 Jan makes this shape pattern using triangles and squares.

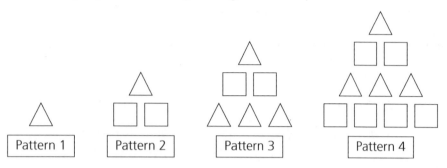

| Pattern 1 | Pattern 2 | Pattern 3 | Pattern 4 |

Callum says Jan will need six triangles and nine squares for the 5th pattern.

Do you agree? Explain your reasoning.

Challenge 2

 5 Toni and Emma both have a number square but something has been spilled on Emma's. Look closely at each number square. Can you explain what is the same and what is different?

−12	−6	0	6
12	18	24	30
36	42		54
60			

9	18	27	36
45	54	63	72
81	90	99	108

 6 Use different first terms and make as many different number sequences using the rule 'add or subtract 6' as you can. How many different number sequences can you find where the terms:

a) are all multiples of 6?

b) are all odd numbers?

c) include positive and negative numbers?

How did you do?

Number and place value

The value of each digit in a number is determined by its place value column.

Example: What is the value of the digit 7 in the number 6475?

What will the number be if rounded to the nearest 10, 100 and 1000?

Use a place value chart to determine the value of each digit.

Thousands	Hundreds	Tens	Ones
6	4	7	5

In the number 6475, the value of the digit 7 is 7 tens (or 70).

When rounding, look closely at the value of the digit to the right of the place value column you are rounding to. Round up if the value of the digit is 5 or more. Round down if the value of the digit is less than 5

- 6475 rounded to the nearest 10 is 6480

- 6475 rounded to the nearest 100 is 6500

- 6475 rounded to the nearest 1000 is 6000

Getting started

1 The value of the largest 4-digit number will have the digit 9 in the thousands column. True or false?

2 Amy, Raj and Jon are playing a place value counter game.

Raj says he has made the number 437 on the place value grid.

Thousands	Hundreds	Tens	Ones
● ● ● ●	● ● ●		● ● ● ● ● ● ●

a) Amy says Raj is incorrect. Do you agree? Explain your reasoning.

b) Jon says if you move a counter from the ones column to the thousands column then the number will be greater than 5000. Do you agree? Explain your reasoning.

3 Look at each statement and decide which amount you would rather have. Explain your reasoning.

a) £1000 less than £4001 or £1000 more than £3888?

b) £1000 more than £284 or £1000 less than £3004?

c) £1000 more than £192 or £1000 less than £2120?

(4) This Roman numerals 100 grid has a hole in the middle!

Jon says LXXV is the largest Roman numeral that is missing from the grid. Sam says XXIV is the smallest Roman numeral that is missing from the grid.

Are they both correct? Explain your reasoning.

I 1	XI 11	XXI 21	XXXI 31	XLI 41	LI 51	LXI 61	LXXI 71	LXXXI 81	XCI 91
II 2	XII 12	XXII 22	XXXII 32	XLII 42	LII 52	LXII 62	LXXII 72	LXXXII 82	XCII 92
III 3	XIII 13	XXIII 23	XXXIII 33	XLIII 43	LIII 53	LXIII 63	LXXIII 73	LXXXIII 83	XCIII 93
IV 4	XIV 14							LXXXIV 84	XCIV 94
V 5	XV 15							LXXXV 85	XCV 95
VI 6	XVI 16							LXXXVI 86	XCVI 96
VII 7	XVII 17							LXXXVII 87	XCVII 97
VIII 8	XVIII 18	XXVIII 28	XXXVIII 38	XLVIII 48	LVIII 58	LXVIII 68	LXXVIII 78	LXXXVIII 88	XCVIII 98
IX 9	XIX 19	XXIX 29	XXXIX 39	XLIX 49	LIX 59	LXIX 69	LXXIX 79	LXXXIX 89	XCIX 99
X 10	XX 20	XXX 30	XL 40	L 50	LX 60	LXX 70	LXXX 80	XC 90	C 100

(5) Mr and Mrs Khan want to buy a new car. They want to look at cars that cost approximately £9000

Write the letters of the cars they will look at.

Car for sale		
	Name	**Price**
A	Fredro	£9876
B	Beano	£9175
C	Greft	£8689
D	Denby	£9910
E	Evie	£8910

 (6) Some of the ways that the number 5432 can be expressed are:

- 5 thousands, 4 hundreds, 3 tens, 2 ones
- 54 hundreds, 3 tens, 2 ones
- 543 tens and 2 ones

How many different ways can you find to express the number 8670?

(7) What is the same and what is different about these numbers?
Use what you know about the place value of digits and rounding rules.

| 3684 | | 5682 | | 9683 | | 4681 | | 9680 |

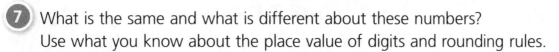

How did you do?

Addition

Remember, you may need to use the column method to complete addition calculations.

Example: Calculate 5617 + 2524 using a formal written method.

To solve the addition calculation you can use this method:

```
    5  6  1  7
+   2  5  2  4
    8  1  4  1
    1     1
```

Remember to:

- use place value to line up the digits correctly
- always calculate from the ones column to the thousands column and carry when needed.

Getting started

 1 Work out which calculations are true and which are false.

Explain the error in the statements that are false.

a) 7070 + 1958 = 9028

b) 2968 + 1304 = 4272

c) 3954 + 3211 = 7165

d) 6894 + 3201 = 9095

e) 1632 + 2493 = 4125

 2 Here are the flight distances from London to Rome and London to Madrid:

- London to Rome: 1434 miles

- London to Madrid: 1264 miles

A pilot flies a plane from London to Madrid. She flies back to London and then on to Rome. What is the total distance that the pilot has travelled?

 3 Belle says the total of two 4-digit numbers will never be greater than one million. Do you agree? Explain your answer.

4 The answer to Harry's calculation is 5250. What could the question be?

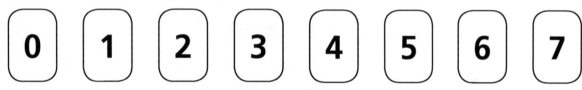

5 Su and Amy are playing 'guess my number'.

Su says: 'I subtract 1290 and I get 3089.'

Amy says: 'My number is 2768 more than Su's number.'

Work out each of their numbers.

Challenge 2

6 Use the digit cards to make two different 4-digit numbers that round to seven thousand when added together.

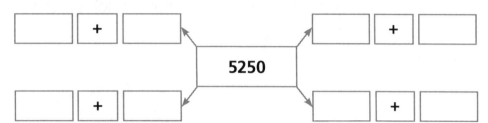

How many different possibilities can you find?

7 Each number block above the base is made up from the sum of the two numbers supporting it.

Copy the pyramid and complete the missing blocks.

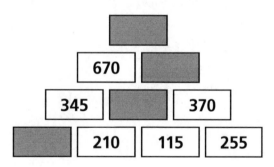

Subtraction

Remember, you may need to use the column method to complete subtraction calculations.

Example: Calculate 3419 − 1253 using a formal written method.

To solve the subtraction calculation you can use this method:

```
       3  1
   3   4  1  9
 − 1   2  5  3
   2   1  6  6
```

Remember to:

– use place value to line up the digits correctly

– always calculate from the ones columns to the thousands and exchange when needed.

Getting started

1. Fairfield School is raising money for charity.

   How much more money do they need to raise to reach their target?

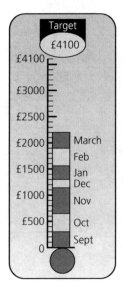

2. Erik has completed four calculations. Work out which are correct and which are incorrect.

   Explain the error in the calculations that are incorrect and give the correct answer.

a)
```
   6  5  9  1
 − 3  2  9  8
   3  7  0  7
```

b)
```
      3  1
   4  2  7  8
 − 1  5  3  6
   2  7  4  2
```

c)
```
      7  1
   3  8  4  9
 − 2  7  5  8
   1  0  8  1
```

d)
```
      5  1
   6  3  4  2
 − 3  7  1  2
   2  6  3  4
```

3 Solve each calculation and identify the odd one out. Explain your reasoning.

a)
```
    5  4  9  7
 -  3  2  6  4
 _____
```

b)
```
    6  9  5  9
 -  4  7  2  6
 _____
```

c)
```
    5  7  1  8
 -  3  4  8  5
 _____
```

d)
```
    8  9  4  6
 -  6  7  1  3
 _____
```

4 Bella says that if you keep on subtracting one thousand, two hundred and five from 7850 you will get to 3030 after five subtraction calculations. Do you agree? Explain your reasoning.

5 Ben and Jack are playing 'guess my number'.

Ben says: 'I add 1547 and I get the number 8324.'

Jack says: 'My number is 3526 less than Ben's number.'

Work out each of their numbers.

6 Use four of the digit cards to create a subtraction and then work out the answer.

7   3   2

1   9   9

```
    9    9    9    9
 -  ▢    ▢    ▢    ▢
 _____
```

How many different calculations can you make?

What is the smallest answer you can make? Explain your strategy.

What is the largest answer you can make? Explain your strategy.

7 If there is a digit 6 in the tens column when subtracting two 4-digit numbers, then you have to exchange a hundred. Is this always true, sometimes true or never true?

How did you do?

Addition and subtraction

Remember that addition and subtraction are the inverse of one another.

Example: Molly calculates 4456 + 2369 and must then check her calculation using the inverse operation.

```
    4  4  5  6              7  11  1
 +  2  3  6  9           6  8̶  2̶  5
    6  8  2  5        -  2  3  6  9
       1  1              4  4  5  6
```

Getting started

1 Ali says you need to use the = symbol to complete this number sentence.

Tara says you need to use the > symbol.

7632 − 5489 ☐ 1889 + 996

Who do you agree with? Explain your reasoning.

2 If the answer is 4596, what could the question be? Use only addition and subtraction.

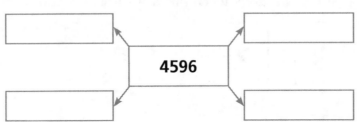

4596

3 Jay completes two addition calculations and then checks his calculations using the inverse. Are his inverse calculations correct? Explain any errors he has made.

a)
```
    5  1  9  8           7  6  6  7
 +  2  4  6  9        -  2  4  6  9
    7  6  6  7           5  2  0  2
       1  1
```

b)
```
    6  0  4  9              6  1
 +  3  6  2  5           9  6  7̶  4
    9  6  7  4        -  6  0  4  9
          1             3  6  2  5
```

4 Write down all the different possible addition and subtraction calculations represented by each bar model.

a)

2775	
1706	1069

b)

3854	5321
9175	

c)

6698	
3819	2879

5 Here is a magic square. Each row, column and diagonal equals the same magic number.

Find the magic number and then calculate the missing numbers.

1352		2028
	2366	
2704		

6 In this diagram, the numbers in the triangles add together to make the number in the circle. The number in the square is 2980 less than the number in the circle.

Use these rules to calculate the missing numbers in these diagrams.

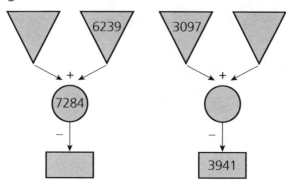

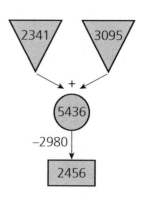

How did you do?

43

Multiplication

To complete multiplication calculations, you may want to use the short multiplication method.

Example: There are 365 nails in one jar. How many nails are in seven jars?

To solve this problem you can use this method:

```
      3   6   5
  ×           7
  2   5   5   5
      4   3
```

Remember to:

– use place value to line up the digits correctly

– always calculate from the ones column to the thousands and carry when needed.

Getting started

 1 Work out which calculations are true and which are false.

a) 39 × 7 = 30 × 7 + 9 × 7

b) 58 × 9 = 60 × 9 – 8 × 9

c) 24 × 6 = 10 × 6 + 10 × 6 + 4 + 6

d) 77 × 5 = 60 × 5 + 10 × 5 + 7 × 5

 2 Calculate the missing numbers in this times table grid.

×	7	12
	63	
4		
		96

 3 Each shelf in Jiffy Supermarket can hold 589 tins.

How many tins can be stacked on six shelves?

Challenge 1

4 Zoe says 98 × 6 is the same as 100 × 6 – 1 × 6

Do you agree? Explain your reasoning.

5 Look at these two calculations. What is the same and what is different?

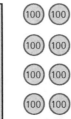

	2	6	5
×			4
1	0	6	0
	2	2	

800 + 240 + 20 = 1060

Challenge 2

6 Use the numbers on the digit cards to create a multiplication. Then work out the answer.

How many different calculations can you make?

What is the largest product you can make? Explain your strategy.

4 **8** **9** **7**

×

_____

_____

7 Crack the times table code and find the value of each letter.

J × J = CD   D × J = J   B × J = EA

C × J = AE   K × J = BF   A × J = FB

E × J = DC   F × J = HK   H × J = KH

How did you do?

Division

To complete division calculations, you may want to use the short division method.

Example: There are six ball pits. 906 balls are distributed equally between each of the ball pits. How many balls are in each pit?

$$\begin{array}{r} 1\ 5\ 1 \\ \hline 6\overline{)9\ \overset{3}{0}\ 6} \end{array}$$

Remember to:

– use your times table facts to help

– carry over the remainder to the next place value column.

Getting started

 1 Look at these division calculations. Find the odd one out. Explain your reasoning.

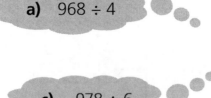 **a)** 968 ÷ 4

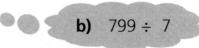 **b)** 799 ÷ 7

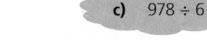 **c)** 978 ÷ 6

 2 Some groups of friends each win a sum of money. Decide which group you would most like to be part of. Explain your reasoning.

Group A
£189 shared between three friends

Group B
£275 shared between five friends

Group C
£288 shared between nine friends

Group D
£266 shared between seven friends

 3 The headteacher needs to buy 495 new pencils for all the pupils in the school. Pencils are sold in packs of nine. The head thinks she needs to buy 55 packs.

Do you agree? Explain your reasoning.

4 The number in the top box is the product of the two numbers below it. Calculate the missing numbers.

a)

483	
	7

b)

712	
	8

c)

522	
9	

 5 Identify which word problem **cannot** be solved using the calculation below.

$$378 \div 7 = 54$$

a) There are seven jars that have 54 marbles in each jar. How many marbles are there altogether?

b) 378 roses are sold to seven different flower shops. How many roses are sold to each flower shop?

c) A coach holds 54 passengers. How many passengers will seven coaches hold?

d) There are 378 pennies in each of the seven children's money boxes. How much money is there in total?

Challenge 2

6 Leyla puts 68 seeds in each of her pots. She uses seven pots and has four seeds left over.

Leyla says she started with 748 seeds. Explain why Leyla is incorrect and the error she has made.

7 $120 \div 9$ is 13 remainder 3

Investigate other 2-digit and 3-digit numbers that have a remainder of 3 when divided by 9

Can you describe any patterns or find any rules?

What if you had a remainder of 5 when you divided by 9? Can you use the rule you found for 'divide by 9 and remainder 3'?

How did you do?

Multiplication and division

Remember that multiplication and division are the inverse of one another.

Getting started

1 Solve these word problems.

a) Gita has 27 bricks. Sami has 8 times more. How many more bricks does Sami have than Gita?

b) The theme park builds a model tower that is 3m high. The height of the real tower is 198m. How many times smaller is the model than the real tower?

c) An oak tree is nine times smaller than the height of The Shard in London. The Shard is 306m high. What is the height of the oak tree?

2 Emma is making a fruit salad with three different fruits. The fruit salad has to have one red fruit, one yellow fruit and one green fruit. Here is the list of fruits Emma can choose from.

Red fruit	Yellow fruit	Green fruit
Watermelon	Banana	Kiwi
Cherries	Pineapple	Green grapes
Raspberries		
Strawberries		

How many different fruit salads can she make? Find all the different possible combinations.

3 Find the rule to make the number in the triangle. Work out the missing numbers.

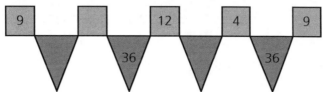

9   12   4   9

36   36

4 Use your multiplication and division facts to work out the value of each symbol and the missing row and column totals.

							41	
80	★	★	★	★	★	★	△	
	★						△	
	★	●	●	△	●	△	△	?
	★						△	
	●	●	●	●	●	●	●	63
	?							

5 The length of a small patio is 210cm. There is a fence on each side of the patio. One fence is divided into three equal panels. The other is divided into five equal panels.

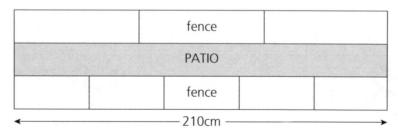

	fence	
PATIO		
	fence	

⟵——————— 210cm ———————⟶   Not actual size

What is the length of one panel in each of the fences?

6 Are these statements true or false? Explain your reasoning.

a) There are 84 sweets altogether. Ricky has three times as many sweets as Charlie. Ricky says he has 56 sweets and Charlie says he has 28 sweets.

b) Jess has eight times as many cards as Amelia. Together they have 207 cards. Amelia has 23 cards and Jess has 184 cards.

How did you do?

Fractions 1

Remember that a fraction is part of a whole number.

Example: There are a number of different ways to add fractions. For example, you can use a fraction bar.

$$\frac{4}{6} + \frac{5}{6} = \frac{9}{6}$$

$$\frac{9}{6}$$

A fraction wall can help you find equivalent fractions.

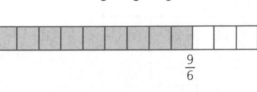

1 whole							
$\frac{1}{2}$				$\frac{1}{2}$			
$\frac{1}{3}$		$\frac{1}{3}$			$\frac{1}{3}$		
$\frac{1}{4}$		$\frac{1}{4}$		$\frac{1}{4}$		$\frac{1}{4}$	
$\frac{1}{5}$	$\frac{1}{5}$		$\frac{1}{5}$		$\frac{1}{5}$		$\frac{1}{5}$
$\frac{1}{6}$	$\frac{1}{6}$	$\frac{1}{6}$	$\frac{1}{6}$	$\frac{1}{6}$	$\frac{1}{6}$		
$\frac{1}{8}$	$\frac{1}{8}$	$\frac{1}{8}$	$\frac{1}{8}$	$\frac{1}{8}$	$\frac{1}{8}$	$\frac{1}{8}$	$\frac{1}{8}$

Getting started

1 Work out which calculations are true and which are false.

a) $\frac{1}{4} + \frac{5}{4} = \frac{6}{4}$

b) $\frac{8}{9} + \frac{3}{9} = \frac{13}{9}$

c) $\frac{3}{5} + \frac{5}{5} + \frac{4}{5} = \frac{12}{5}$

d) $\frac{6}{7} - \frac{2}{7} - \frac{1}{7} = \frac{4}{7}$

2 Look at these pictures. What is the same? What is different?

3 Gregor and Benita are finding equivalent fractions.

Gregor looks at these two diagrams and says: 'Two-quarters is the same as seven-eighths.'

Benita agrees as she says: 'The lengths of the shaded parts are equal to one another.'

Do you agree? Explain your reasoning.

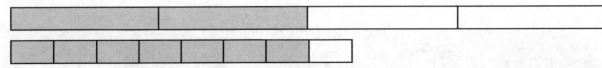

4 Look at each statement. Explain which amount you would rather have.

a) $\frac{3}{8}$ of £256   or $\frac{2}{3}$ of £102?

b) $\frac{7}{9}$ of £126   or $\frac{9}{12}$ of £144?

c) $\frac{4}{6}$ of £324   or $\frac{2}{7}$ of £392?

5 Copy the diagram and shade $\frac{2}{3}$ of the sections.

How many different ways can you find to do this?

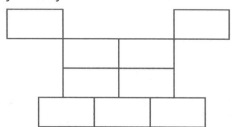

6 Work out the numerators to make the number sentence correct.

Find at least three different answers.

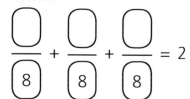

$$\frac{\bigcirc}{8} + \frac{\bigcirc}{8} + \frac{\bigcirc}{8} = 2$$

7 Each letter represents a different digit. 0 (zero) is represented by the letter O.

Solve the puzzle to discover what each letter represents.

$\frac{1}{2}$ of E = $\frac{1}{2}$ E = ☐

$\frac{1}{2}$ of EO = A   O = 0

$\frac{1}{2}$ of F = E   A = ☐

$\frac{1}{2}$ of EF = D   F = ☐

$\frac{1}{2}$ of D = G   D = ☐

                       G = ☐

How did you do?

Fractions 2

Remember that a fraction can be represented as a decimal number because they are both parts of a whole.

Examples:

Divide 4 by 10 and 100. Give your answer as a fraction and a decimal.

$4 \div 10 = \frac{4}{10} = 0.4$

$4 \div 100 = \frac{4}{100} = 0.04$

Divide 24 by 10 and 100

	T	O	.	$\frac{1}{10}$	$\frac{1}{100}$
	2	4			
÷10		2	.	4	
÷100		0	.	2	4

Round 1.7 to the nearest whole number.

1.7 rounded to the nearest whole number is 2.

Remember the rounding rules: if the digit to the right of the place value column that you are rounding is less than 5, then round down; if it is 5 or more, round up!

Getting started

1. Find the rule. Then work out the missing numbers in the number sequence.

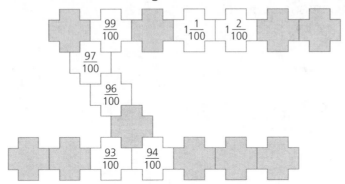

2. Cheryl says that, if she rounds each number to the nearest whole number, an approximate answer to the calculation 5.9 + 6.6 is 12
Do you agree? Explain your reasoning.

3. Which is the odd one out?

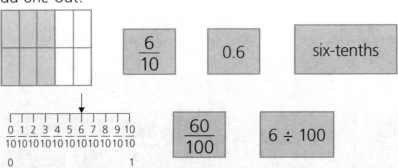

4 Use these digit cards to make each number sentence correct. Find as many different ways as possible.

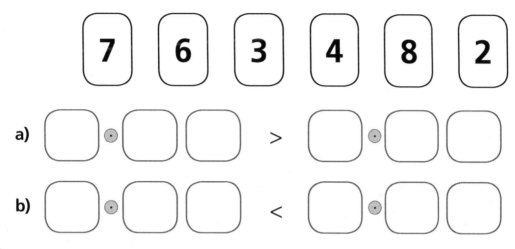

a) ⬜.⬜⬜ > ⬜.⬜⬜

b) ⬜.⬜⬜ < ⬜.⬜⬜

5 Decide if each statement is always true, sometimes true or never true.

a) A decimal number with 6 ones and 5 tenths will be smaller than a decimal number with 8 ones and 3 tenths.

b) A decimal number with 8 tenths will round down to the nearest whole number.

c) A decimal number with 2 tenths will always be greater than a decimal number with 2 hundredths.

Challenge 2

6 Katy starts with a 2-digit multiple of 6. She divides the multiple by 10 and has an odd number of ones and an even number of tenths.

List all the possible multiples of 6 under 80 that Katy could have divided.

7 Osama picked four different decimal numbers. Use the clues to find out which four decimal numbers he picked.

Clues:

- One of the numbers is equivalent to $\frac{1}{4}$

- The largest number is 0.1 more than $\frac{3}{5}$

- The smallest number is 0.15 less than $\frac{1}{5}$

- The remaining number is three-tenths less than the largest number.

How did you do?

Measures 1

Remember that converting measures involves multiplying and dividing by 10, 100 and 1000

Examples:

Convert 6.35 litres into millilitres.	Convert 2.5km into metres.	Convert $4\frac{1}{4}$kg into grams.
×1000 = 6350 millilitres	×1000 = 2500 metres	×1000 = 4250 grams

			6	.	3	5
6	3	5	0	.	0	0

			2	.	5	0
2	5	0	0	.	0	0

			4	.	2	5
4	2	5	0	.	0	0

Getting started

1 Look at each statement. Decide which are true and which are false. Explain your reasoning.

a) 3kg = 3000g   b) 7.5 litre < 7050mL

c) 400g > 0.5kg   d) 1.75m = 175cm

e) 1.4km > 1000m   f) 6546mL < 6.5 litres

2 Lily's school bag weighs a quarter of a kilogram when it is empty.

Lily puts five identical books in the bag and it now weighs $1\frac{3}{4}$kg.

How much does each book weigh?

3 It is a hot day and you are feeling very thirsty. Which amount of drink would you rather have? Explain your reasoning.

| $\frac{1}{4}$ litre | | 2005mL | | $\frac{2}{5}$ of 5 litres | | $\frac{3}{4}$ of 3 litres |

4 The route map below shows the distances between city check points on a cycle race.

Use the map to find the half-way distance between Exeter and York along the cycle route.

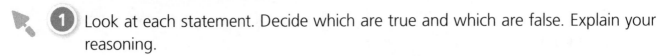

York

Derby

106km

Bristol

215km

Exeter

130km

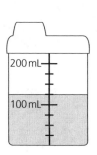

5 Here is a baby's drinking cup.

The baby has drunk what is missing from this cup plus three full cups.

How much has the baby drunk altogether? Give your answer in litres.

6 Jackson needs 15 litres of water to wash the car. He decides to fill up his 15-litre bucket using a bottle, a jug and a bowl. Find at least three different ways Jackson can fill his bucket using these containers.

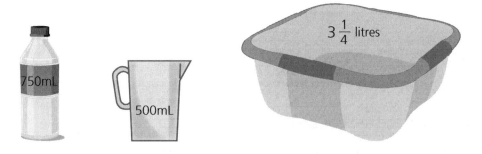

$3\frac{1}{4}$ litres

750mL

500mL

Challenge 2

7 Ella has three measuring jugs.

- The first jug is the smallest jug and holds 3 litres.
- The second jug is $1\frac{1}{2}$ times larger than the first jug.
- The third jug is $1\frac{1}{2}$ times larger than the second jug.

Ella thinks the capacity of the third jug is 9 litres. Explain why she is incorrect.

8 Work out the missing measures so that each line gives a total mass of 5kg.

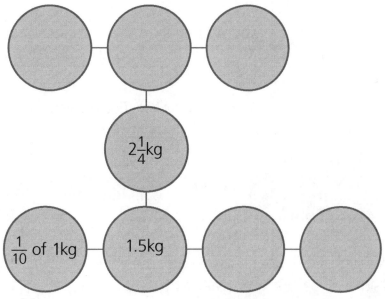

$2\frac{1}{4}$kg

$\frac{1}{10}$ of 1kg

1.5kg

How did you do?

Remember that the units of length are millimetres, centimetres, metres and kilometres

Example: The perimeter is the total distance around a shape. The area of a shape is how much surface it has.

Perimeter: 6cm + 6cm + 12cm + 12cm = 36cm

Area: 6cm × 12cm = 72cm²

Getting started

1. Calculate the area of each shape to find the odd one out.

   The shapes are drawn on centimetre-squared paper.

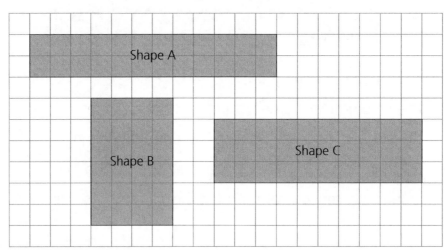

Shape A

Shape B

Shape C

2. Mrs Drew is making the display boards for the corridor. There is a display board for each of the three classes. She needs to add a ribbon border around the perimeter of each board.

   What is the total length of ribbon that Mrs Drew needs to complete the border? Give your answer in metres.

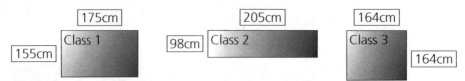

175cm

Class 1

155cm

205cm

Class 2

98cm

164cm

Class 3

164cm

3. The perimeter of a rectangle is 102cm. The shortest side is 18cm so Liv says the longest side will be 66cm. Explain why Liv is incorrect.

4 Mac wants to rent an allotment. He has two to choose from. If he wants the largest amount of space possible, which will he choose and why?

Allotment A is 7m by 12m.   Allotment B is 9m by 7m.

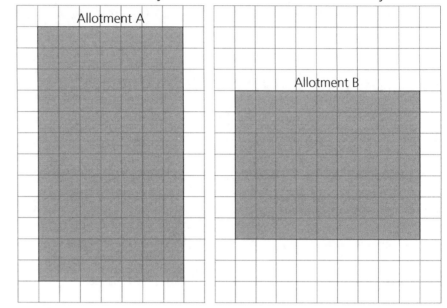

 5 Rhianna says the perimeter of a rectangle will be greater than the perimeter of a square if one side is longer than the side of the square and one side is shorter. Is this always, sometimes or never true?

 6 Gary is having a new patio. He would like a range of designs to present to his builder.

Using 1cm squared paper, draw as many rectilinear patios with an area of 36cm^2 as possible.

 7 Hope says it is impossible to draw a square with an area of 63cm^2 where the side of the square is a whole number of centimetres.

Is she correct? Explain your reasoning.

8 These rectangular tiles are four times as long as they are wide.

What is the perimeter of the centre square?

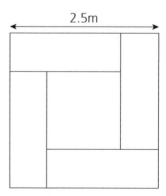

2.5m

 **How did you do?**

Money

Remember that the units pounds (£) and pence (p) are used for money in the UK.

> **Example:** Amy buys a t-shirt for £4.75 and a pair of jeans for £10.99
>
> How much change will she get from £20?
>
> £4.75 + £10.99 = £15.74
>
> £20.00 − £15.74 = £4.26
>
> Amy will get £4.26 change.

Getting started

1 Decide if each statement is true or false.

a) £5.65 > £5.60   b) £6.99 < £6.89

c) £7.98 < £7.69   d) £4.50 = £3.75 + £1.25

e) £6.50 < $\frac{1}{2}$ of £15

2 Joel spends £9.85 on a cinema ticket, £1.70 on a drink and £4.25 on a medium box of popcorn. How much would he have saved if he had bought a cinema package to match the items he chose?

Package A Cinema ticket + drink	£11.00
Package B Cinema ticket + drink + medium box of popcorn	£15.00
Package C Cinema ticket + drink + medium box of popcorn + hot dog	£17.50

3 Beth and Oscar both buy 12 cans of lemonade.

- Beth buys three packs of four cans.
- Oscar buys two packs of six cans.

£2.60

£2.88

Oscar tells Beth that she paid more per can than he did. What do you think? Explain your reasoning.

4 The table shows the prices to hire a boat.

Motor boats	Rowing boats
£1.50 for 15 minutes	£2.50 for 1 hour

a) Ryan pays £4.50 to hire a motor boat. He goes out at 1.35pm. By what time must he return?

b) How much does it cost to hire a rowing boat for 2.5 hours?

5 Here is a magic square involving money. Each row, column and diagonal equals the same magic number. Find the magic number and then work out the missing numbers.

£4.48		
£1.68		£3.92
£2.24	£5.04	

6 Joe paid £15 for three presents: A, B and C.

- For A and B he paid a total of £8
- For B and C he paid a total of £12
- For A and C he paid a total of £10

How much did Joe pay for each present?

7 Sid and Sara share this amount of money.

Sid gets three times as much as Sara so he says he needs to take a £1 coin, a 50p coin and a 20p coin.

Is he correct? Explain your reasoning.

8 Pippa says she would rather have $\frac{2}{3}$ of the money in Set 1 because it has more coins than Set 2. Which set would you rather have $\frac{2}{3}$ of?

Set 1   **Set 2**

How did you do?

Time

Remember that time uses the units hours, minutes and seconds.

Example: It is Saturday afternoon. This analogue clocks shows that it is twenty-two minutes to five in the afternoon.

These digital clocks also show twenty-two minutes to five.

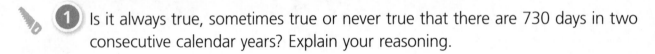

Getting started

1. Is it always true, sometimes true or never true that there are 730 days in two consecutive calendar years? Explain your reasoning.

2. Look at each set of times. Identify the odd one out. Explain your reasoning.

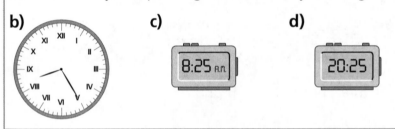

Set 1 a) It is twenty-five past eight on Saturday evening.

b)   c) 8:25 A.M.   d) 20:25

Set 2 a) It is half-past six on Monday morning.

b)   c) 6:30 A.M.   d) 18:30

3. Day 1 of the cricket tournament starts at 09:30 and finishes at 18:00. There are three 25-minute intervals during the tournament and a 55-minute lunch break. How long were the cricketers playing for?

4. Noah said: 'I ran the race in 312 seconds, so I am faster than Bes who ran the race in 5 minutes 5 seconds.'

    Bes said: 'That's not true as I ran the race 7 seconds faster than Noah.'

    Who do you agree with? Explain your reasoning.

5 Look at this set of times. What is the same and what is different?

| 7:35pm | twenty-five to eight in the evening | 19:35 |

| thirty-five minutes past seven |

6 Here is a timetable of tours in the city of Curingham.

Tour	Starts	Ends
Museum	9:00	09:45
Cathedral	9:45	11:55
Castle	10:35	11:05
Cave	11:50	11:57

Read each statement. Which are true and which are false? Explain your reasoning.

a) The tour of the castle is 15 minutes shorter than the tour of the museum.

b) The tour of the cave only takes 360 seconds.

c) The tour of the cathedral lasts $\frac{1}{3}$ of 6 hours.

d) The total length of all the tours is 4 hours 2 minutes.

7 Look at each statement and decide which you would rather have. Explain your reasoning.

a) Watch TV for 35 minutes or $\frac{1}{6}$ of 4 hours.

b) Play on the computer for $\frac{1}{10}$ of 65 minutes or 300 seconds.

8 A cake takes 40 minutes to cook in the oven.

Dad says when he gets back from football at 14:15, he must put the cake in the oven so that it is ready to take out of the oven no later than 15:30

Find at least three different times that he can put the cake in the oven.

How did you do?

Properties of shapes

Remember that a 2-D shape is a flat shape.

Example: A rectangle is a 2-D shape and can be described by its shape properties. A rectangle has four right angles. The opposite sides of the rectangle are parallel and of equal length. This is a four-side shaped, so it is a quadrilateral.

Getting started

 1 Look at the shapes in this set. What is the same? What is different?

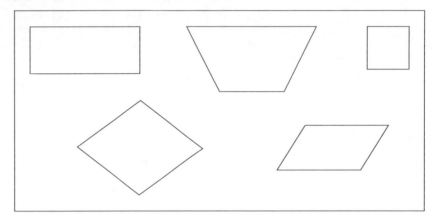

 2 Decide whether these statements are always true, sometimes true or never true. Explain your reasoning.

a) An equilateral triangle has three sides that are the same length and three angles that are the same size.

b) An isosceles triangle has a right angle.

c) A scalene triangle has at least two sides that are the same length.

d) A right-angled triangle has one angle that is 90°.

 3 Wadha says none of these angles are obtuse angles. What do you think? Explain your reasoning.

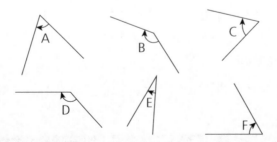

4. Ruby, Tom and Sam are playing 'guess my quadrilateral'.

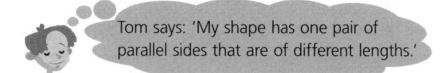

Ruby says: 'My shape has two pairs of equal sides and parallel sides.'

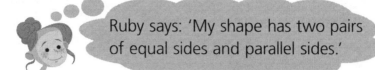

Tom says: 'My shape has one pair of parallel sides that are of different lengths.'

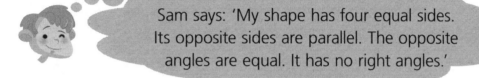

Sam says: 'My shape has four equal sides. Its opposite sides are parallel. The opposite angles are equal. It has no right angles.'

Write the name of the shape that each person has.

5. **a)** How many different types of triangles can you create on this geoboard?

   b) How many different types of quadrilaterals can you create on a geoboard like this one?

6. Meg says that to complete this symmetrical pattern, you need to shade the squares where she has put two crosses. Do you agree? Explain your reasoning.

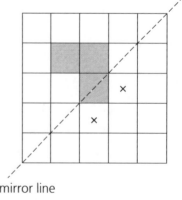

mirror line

7. Investigate how many lines of symmetry each regular polygon has.

Can you spot a pattern? Explain your findings.

How did you do?

63

Position and direction

Remember that a coordinate is the position of a point on a grid. A translation is a 'slide' of a shape using the directions up, down, left or right.

Examples:

a) Write the coordinates of points B and D.

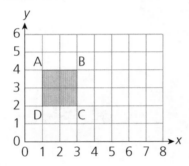

B = (3, 4) and D = (1, 2)

b) Translate the shape 4 squares right and 1 square down.

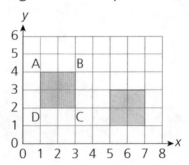

Getting started

1 Here is a map of an island. Look at each statement and decide if it is true or false.

  a) The treasure is at coordinate (5, 3).

  b) The mountain peak is at coordinate (4, 3).

  c) The waterfall is at coordinate (1, 1).

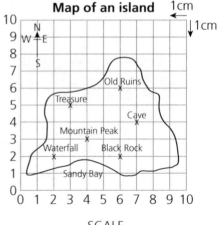

Map of an island

SCALE
1cm to 1km

2 Look at the coordinates for this square. What is the same and what is different about the coordinates?

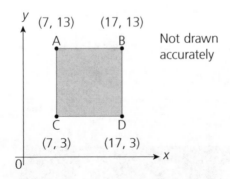

Not drawn accurately

3 A, B, C and D are the vertices of a rectangle.

A and B are shown on the grid.

Point D is (3, 4) so Finn says point C is (2, 5).

Do you agree? Explain your reasoning.

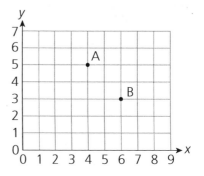

4 Here is a quadrilateral on a square grid.

The quadrilateral is translated so that point A moves to point B.

Charlotte says that point A moves along the same number of squares to the right as it does up.

Do you agree? Explain your reasoning.

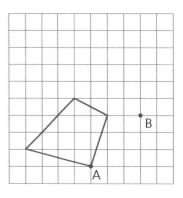

 5 Draw a simple rectilinear shape on centimetre-squared paper.

Then translate the shape four times using a rule you have made up.

Look at the pattern of the coordinates of one vertex and predict the 10th term.

For example, the translation rule for this pattern is 3 right and 1 up. This is reflected in the coordinates for each shape:

Shape 1, point A = (3, 3)

Shape 2, point A = (6, 4)

Shape 3, point A = (9, 5)

Shape 4, point A = (12, 6) ...

Shape 10, point A = (30, 12)

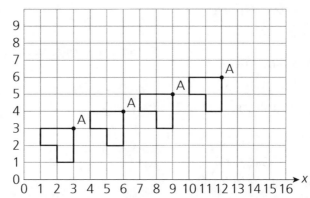

How did you do?

Statistics

Remember, data in charts tells us information.

Example:

A pictogram uses pictures or symbols to display information. You need to look carefully at the key to find the value of each symbol.

Bar charts use blocks and bars to show information. The blocks and bars can be vertical or horizontal.

A time graph shows information that has been collected over a period of time.

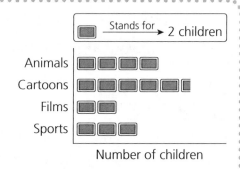

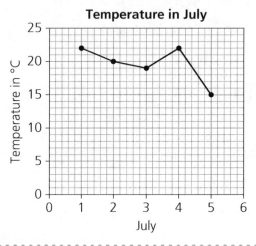

Getting started

1. Interpret the pictogram. Decide which of the statements are true and which are false.

   a) There are two strawberry lollipops for sale.

   b) There are nine more lime fizz lollipops than strawberry lollipops.

   c) There are 45 fewer iceflake lollipops than sunshine yellow lollipops.

   d) There are 108 lollipops for sale in total at the sweet shop.

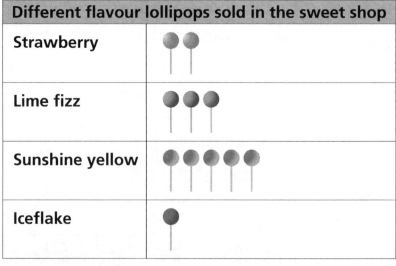

Different flavour lollipops sold in the sweet shop

Key: represents 9 lollipops

2 This table shows the numbers of children who took part in different outdoor activities over the summer holiday.

Lexi says: 'Sailing is my favourite activity so the chart must show that this was the most popular outdoor activity.'

Explain why Lexi is incorrect.

Outdoor activities done by children

	May	June	July
Walking	40	85	102
Sailing	22	57	30
Climbing	27	32	11

3 Interpret the bar chart and answer these problems.

How pupils get to school

a) How many pupils travel to school by car?

b) How many more travel to school by train than tram?

c) Which two transport modes total the same number as the number of pupils who travel to school by bus?

d) What is the difference in the number of pupils who walk and the number who take transport?

4 Jenna thinks that the depth of the bath stayed the same for 10 minutes.

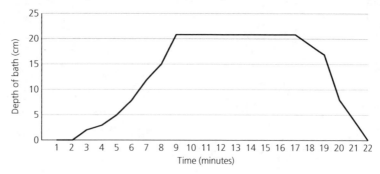

Is she correct? Explain your reasoning.

How did you do?

End-of-year test

1 Ben says that the number 8542 can be expressed as: 8 thousands, 5 hundreds, 4 tens and 2 ones.

Find three different ways to express the number 8542.

2 Darius and Jelena are playing 'guess my number'. Darius says: 'I subtract 1190 and I get 4097.' Jelena says: 'My number is 3426 less than Darius's number.' Work out each of their numbers.

3 Dhruv says that, if there is a digit 8 in the tens column when subtracting two 4-digit numbers, then you exchange a hundred to complete the calculation. Is this always true, sometimes true or never true?

4 A model tower is 6m high. How many times smaller is the model than the real tower if the real tower is 306m high?

5 Dan and Elle are finding equivalent fractions.

Dan looks at these two diagrams and says: 'One-half is the same as three-eighths.'

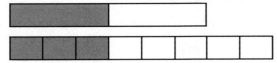

Elle agrees as she thinks the shaded amounts are equal to one another.

Do you agree with Elle and Dan? Explain your reasoning.

6 Which amount would you rather have? Explain why.

$\frac{4}{9}$ of £324 or $\frac{2}{3}$ of £189

7 Identify the odd one out in each set of numbers. Explain your reasoning.

a)
1547
4841
5646
9940
8945
2678

b)
2641
2719
291
2967
2678
2875

8 Look at the following three charts. What is the same and what is different?

Roses	IIII
Daisies	III
Tulips	IIII
Pansies	IIII
Other	IHIT

Flowers	Number
Roses	4
Daisies	3
Tulips	4
Pansies	4
Other	5

Numbers of different types of flowers

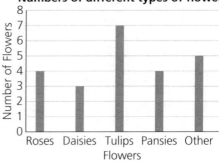

9 Work out the numerators to make the number sentence correct.

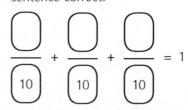

10 Emma makes this sequence using matchsticks.

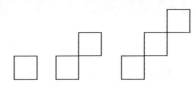

How many matchsticks are needed for the 10th term in the sequence?

11 Look at these shapes. What is the same? What is different?

12 Here is a magic square. Each row, column and diagonal equals the magic number.

Work out the magic number and then calculate the missing numbers.

160		
460	340	220
400		520

13 Would you rather have £1000 less than £2001 or £1000 more than £1101? Explain your reasoning.

14 The answer to Ravi's calculation is 5250. What could the question be?

15 Use the digit cards to complete the number sentence correctly in three different ways.

16 Calculate the area of each shape to find the odd one out.

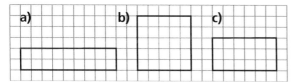

17 Zoe says it is impossible to draw a square with an area of 27cm² where the side is a whole number of centimetres. Is she correct? Explain your reasoning.

18 Tia and Osma both buy 18 cans of cola.

Tia buys 3 packs of 6 cans. Osma buys 9 packs of 2 cans.

£7.50   £1.50

Osma tells Tia that she paid more per can than he did. What do you think? Explain your reasoning.

19 The table shows the prices to hire a boat.

Motor boats	Rowing boats
£1.50 for 15 minutes	£2.50 for 1 hour

Mike pays £8.75 to hire a rowing boat. He goes out onto the water at quarter to two in the afternoon. By what time must he return? Give your answer in 24-hour digital clock format.

20 Look at this set of times. Which is the odd one out?

- 8:35pm
- twenty-five to eight in the evening
- 20:35 • thirty-five minutes past eight

21 Lilly puts 32 seeds in each of her pots. She uses 6 pots and has 4 seeds left over.

Lilly says she started with 196 seeds. Do you agree? Explain your reasoning.

22 Write down all the different possible addition and subtraction calculations to represent the bar model.

4095	
1560	2535

23 To complete this number sentence, Tom says you need to use the = symbol. Tara says you need to use the > symbol. Who do you agree with? Explain your reasoning.

3904 – 672 ◯ 1889 + 299

24 Is it always true, sometimes true or never true that the value of the largest 4-digit number will have the digit 9 in the thousands column?

25 Find the rule for each number sequence. Then continue the pattern for the next five terms in the sequence.

a) 0, 6, 12, 18 ...

b) 0, 25, 50, 75 ...

26 Decide whether each statement is true or false. Explain your reasoning.

a) An equilateral triangle has two angles of equal size and one angle of a different size.

b) An isosceles triangle has three sides that are equal length.

c) A scalene triangle has three different size angles.

27 Mrs Chen needs to buy 685 new pencils for all the pupils in the school. Pencils are sold in packs of 8. Mrs Chen says she needs to buy 85 packs. Do you agree? Explain your reasoning.

28 Errol is thinking about buying a new car. He wants to look at cars that cost approximately £6000

Car for sale		
	Name	**Price**
A	Fredro	£6876
B	Beano	£6175
C	Greft	£7689
D	Denby	£5910
E	Evie	£6499

Write the letters of the cars that he looks at.

29 Identify the odd one out in this set of angles.

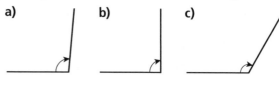

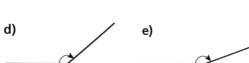

30 Use your multiplication and division facts to work out the value of each symbol.

							75	
61	★	★	★	★	★	★	△	
	★						△	
	★	●	●	△	●	△	△	3081

Mathematical games

Crooked rules

A game for groups of three

You will need:
- A paperclip
- Spinner A*
- Playing board A*
- A pencil

*See the Resources section for a sample spinner and playing board that can be edited, enlarged and photocopied.

1. Take turns to spin the spinner.

2. Write the number you spun in any of the place value columns on the playing board. You can write the number in your own row or in one of your opponents' rows.

3. Carry on until all the place value columns are filled and each player has a 4-digit number in their row.

4. Together, reason and explain which is the largest number. The player with the largest number scores one point.

5. Play another five rounds. The player with the most points wins.

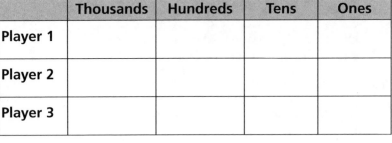

	Thousands	Hundreds	Tens	Ones
Player 1				
Player 2				
Player 3				

Times tables speed

A game for two players

You will need:
- A paperclip
- Spinner B*
- Playing board B*
- Counters in two different colours

*See the Resources section for a sample spinner and playing board that can be edited, enlarged and photocopied.

1. Player A spins the spinner twice and writes down the numbers they spun.

2. Player A multiplies the two digits and covers the product on the playing board with one of their counters.

3. Player B does the same.

4. Players continue to take turns to multiply digits and cover numbers. The first player to get six counters in a row wins.

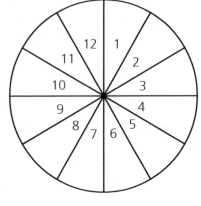

72	42	90	24	33	132	35
14	36	32	40	44	12	48
55	7	54	108	70	56	120
18	63	45	88	27	9	60
96	8	72	21	49	50	11
80	20	100	16	64	99	18
48	22	132	6	84	10	28

Mathematical games

Largest total!

A game for two players

You will need:

- Two sets of 1–9 digit cards*
- Pencil and paper to solve calculations

*See the Resources section for sample cards that can be edited, enlarged and photocopied.

1	2	3
4	5	6
7	8	9

1. Player 1 shuffles their set of digit cards and places them face down on the table so that they don't know what cards they are selecting.

2. Player 1 chooses six cards and uses these cards to make two 3-digit numbers to add together to try and make the largest possible total.

For example, if Player 1 chooses the digits:

| 1 | 8 | 3 | 9 | 2 | 6 |

then they could make the calculation:

| 3 | 6 | 2 | + | 9 | 1 | 8 |

The total = 1280

3. Player 2 uses the same digits from their own set of cards to try and make a calculation that is larger than Player 1's by reasoning and explaining about the place value of the digits and then proving their explanation with a calculation. If Player 2 succeeds, they score a point; if not, then Player 1 scores.

4. Repeat, but this time swapping roles so Player 2 shuffles and places their digit cards face down and makes the first total.

Creating word problems!

A game for two or more players

You will need:

- Two paper clips
- Two pencils
- Some paper
- Spinner C* and Spinner D*

*See the Resources section for sample spinners that can be edited, enlarged and photocopied.

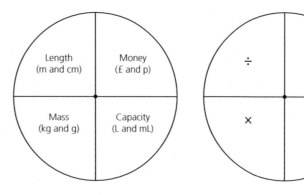

1. Take turns to spin the two spinners.

2. Read the spinners to find out which operation to use and what your problem needs to be about.

3. Make up and write a 'real-life' word problem and then solve the problem together.

For example:
If you spin '+' on Spinner D and 'mass' on Spinner C, then you could make up the following problem:
The mass of Meg's purse is 185g and the mass of her bag is 450g. When Meg puts her purse in the bag, what is the total mass?

Mathematical games

Palindromes

A game for two or more players

Palindromes are numbers that read the same forwards and backwards.

- 737 is a palindrome number because it reads 737 forwards and 737 backwards.
- 234 is not a palindrome number because it reads 432 backwards, which is not the same as 234.

You will need:

- A paperclip
- A pencil
- Paper
- Spinner A*

*See the Resources section for a sample spinner that can be edited, enlarged and photocopied.

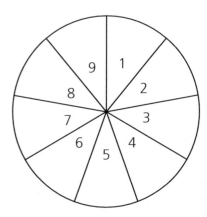

1. Take turns to spin the spinner three times and write down your three digits (e.g. 4, 2, 1).

2. Use the numbers in any order to make a 3-digit number (e.g. 124).

3. Reverse the digits to make another number (e.g. 421).

4. Work out if the number is a palindrome or not. Explain your reasoning.

5. If the number is a palindrome, score a point.

6. The first player to score three points wins.

Moving across the road

A game for two players

You will need:

- Spinner B*
- A paper clip
- A pencil
- Playing board C for each player*

*See the Resources section for a sample spinner and playing board that can be edited, enlarged and photocopied.

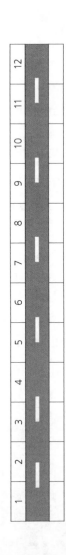

1. Player 1 spins the spinner and circles the number on their playing board that matches the number on the spinner.

2. Player 1 spins the spinner again. This time they multiply the number circled on their playing board by the number shown on the spinner.

3. Player 1 says the answer out loud. If Player 2 agrees with the answer, Player 1 crosses out the number that is circled and writes the answer in the opposite box across the road.

4. Player 2 now has their turn.

5. Keep taking turns. If a player spins a number that has already been moved across the road, they miss a go.

6. The first player to move all their numbers across the road wins.

Guess my shape!

A game for two players

You will need:

- Two pencils
- Paper

1. Player 1 chooses a 2-D or 3-D shape and writes down the name of the chosen shape. This should not be shown to their opponent.

2. Player 2 asks four key questions about the shape's properties. Player 1 answers the questions, using 'yes' or 'no' only.

3. Player 2 tries to guess the name of the shape from the answers given.

4. If Player 2 guesses the correct shape then they score a point.

5. Swap roles.

6. After four goes each, the player with the most points wins.

Adding sixths!

A game for two players

You will need:

- A 1–6 die
- A pencil
- Paper

1. Player 1 rolls the die. The number rolled will be the numerator. As the die has six faces, six will be the denominator for each fraction. So, if you rolled a four, your fraction would be $\frac{4}{6}$

2. Player 1 rolls the die again to make another fraction.

3. Player 2 repeats.

4. Both players add the fractions they created together and write down their answers.

5. The player with the larger number of sixths scores a point.

6. After six rounds, the player with more points wins.

Spinner A

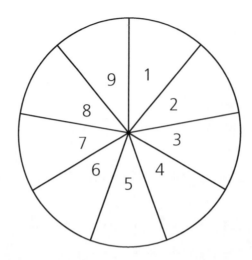

Playing board A

	Thousands	Hundreds	Tens	Ones
Player 1				
Player 2				
Player 3				

Spinner B

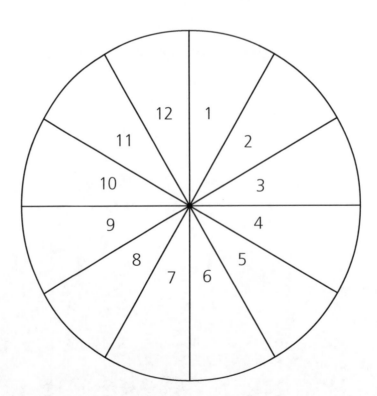

Playing board B

72	42	90	24	33	132	35
14	36	32	40	44	12	48
55	7	54	108	70	56	120
18	63	45	88	27	9	60
96	8	72	21	49	50	11
80	20	100	16	64	99	18
48	22	132	6	84	10	28

1–9 digit cards

1	2	3
4	5	6
7	8	9

Resources

Spinner C

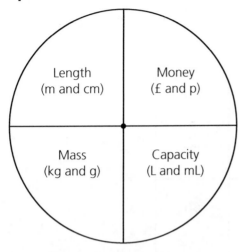

Spinner D

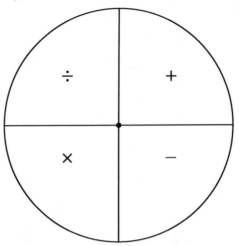

Playing board C

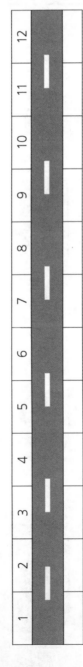

area: the exterior surface of a shape

capacity: how much something holds; metric units for capacity are litres and millilitres

decimal fraction: a fraction expressed as a decimal

denominator: the bottom number of a fraction; tells you how many equal parts the quantity or shape has been divided into. In $\frac{2}{5}$ the denominator is 5

edge: where two or more faces meet in a 3-D shape

equivalent fractions: fractions with the same value as each other, for example, $\frac{1}{4}$ and $\frac{2}{8}$

face: the flat surface of a shape

factor: numbers you can multiply together to get another number, for example, 2 and 3 are factors of 6, because $2 \times 3 = 6$

fraction: a number that is part of a whole number; can be written in many ways, for example, $\frac{3}{4}$ or 0.75

length: the measurement of a line, distance or period of time; metric units for distance are kilometres, metres, centimetres, millimetres; units for time include hours, minutes and seconds

mass: the amount of matter or material in an object; metric units for mass are grams and kilograms

metric units: part of the metric system of measurement. The units are based on tens, hundreds and thousands. Metric units are used for length (millimetre, centimetre, metre, kilometre), mass (gram, kilogram) and capacity (millilitre, litre).

multiple: the result of multiplying a number by an integer, for example, 12 is a multiple of 3 because $3 \times 4 = 12$

net: a pattern that, when cut and folded, will make a 3-D shape

numerator: the top number of a fraction; tells you how many equal parts there are. In $\frac{2}{5}$ the numerator is 2

pattern: an arrangement of numbers, lines or shapes that follows a rule

perimeter: the total distance all the way round a shape

pictogram: a diagram where symbols are used to represent quantities; a symbol can stand for one thing or a number of things

place value: the value of a digit that relates to its position or place in a number

polygon: a shape with at least three sides and angles, usually five or more

prime number: a number that is only divisible by 1 or itself

product: the result of multiplying one number by another, for example, the product of 2 and 3 is 6 since $2 \times 3 = 6$

quadrilateral: a four-sided shape

remainder: in the context of division requiring a whole number answer (quotient), the remainder is the amount left over after the division is completed

vertices: the corners of a shape

Answers: Teaching the strategies

Note: Answers will often vary. Some sample answers are provided for guidance. Teachers should use their judgment when reviewing pupils' responses to open-ended questions and when assessing their reasoning.

Finding all possibilities

1. Rectangle 12cm × 3cm which has an area of 36cm². Any rectilinear shape with an area of 36cm², e.g. square 6 × 6 or rectangle 9 × 4

2.
- Gold trousers, white shirt, silver jacket, black belt
- Gold trousers, white shirt, silver jacket, guitar belt
- Gold trousers, white shirt, stars jacket, black belt
- Gold trousers, white shirt, stars jacket, guitar belt
- Black trousers, white shirt, silver jacket, black belt
- Black trousers, white shirt, silver jacket, guitar belt
- Black trousers, white shirt, stars jacket, black belt
- Black trousers, white shirt, stars jacket, guitar belt
- Purple trousers, white shirt, silver jacket, black belt
- Purple trousers, white shirt, silver jacket, guitar belt
- Purple trousers, white shirt, stars jacket, black belt
- Purple trousers, white shirt, stars jacket, guitar belt

3. Here are four out of the eight possibilities: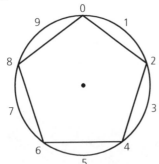

4. 1 × 1 × 48; 1 × 2 × 24; 1 × 3 × 16; 1 × 4 × 12; 1 × 6 × 8; 2 × 2 × 12; 2 × 3 × 8; 2 × 4 × 6; 3 × 4 × 4

5. For example: 89 hundreds and 76 ones; 8 thousands, 97 tens, 6 ones; 8 thousands and 976 ones

6. For example: 4.96 > 4.28, 6.28 > 4.49, 9.24 > 8.64

Finding rules and describing patterns

1. 840, 905, 1000

2. Even number multiplication facts can never have an odd number as the ones place digit. The times tables for two, four, six and eight only hit 2, 4, 6, 8, and 0.

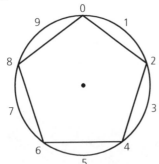

Pupils should observe that the five times table only hits 5 and 0 so it is a straight line.
They should notice that the one, three, seven and nine times tables hit all possible ones place digits.
All even multiplication facts have the same pentagon pattern with corners at 0, 2, 4, 6 and 8.

3. Add 9

4.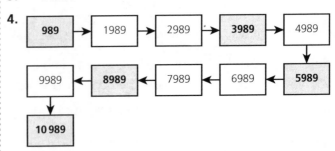

Logic puzzles

1.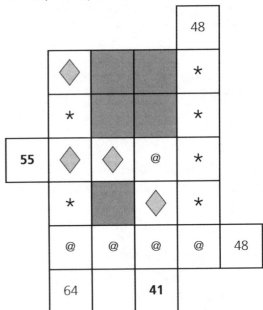

2. @ = 12, ★ = 9, ◇ = 17

				48
	◇			★
	★			★
55	◇	◇	@	★
	★		◇	★
	@	@	@	@	48
	64		41	

3.

		23/8		
	11/8		12/8	
	6/8	5/8	7/8	
4/8	2/8	3/8	4/8	

Answers: Teaching the strategies

4. Sue: 5515, Amy: 6580

Real-life word problems
1. £4.90
2. 15cm²
3. 83m
4. 5 hours 0 minutes
5. 270 cards
6. 20 girls

True or false
1. a) False: because the value of the tenths in each number is different so they cannot be equal.
   b) True: because the value of the tenths column in the first number is 2 tenths, which is smaller than the value of the tenths number in the second number, which is 3 tenths. So 1.24 is smaller than 1.39
   c) True: because the value of the tenths column in the first number is 4 tenths, which is larger than the value of the tenths number in the second number, which is 0 tenths. So 1.49 is greater than 1.08
   d) False: because the value of the tenths column in the first number is 9 tenths, which is larger than the value of the tenths number in the second number, which is 7 tenths. So 1.98 is greater than 1.70

2. a) Incorrect: label should be isosceles
   b) Correct
   c) Incorrect: label should be right-angled triangle
   d) Incorrect: label should be scalene

3. a) Correct
   b) Incorrect: answer should be $\frac{4}{10}$ or $\frac{2}{5}$
   c) Incorrect: answer should be $\frac{6}{5}$ or $1\frac{1}{5}$
   d) Correct

4. a) True
   b) False: $\frac{2}{12} = \frac{1}{6}$
   c) True
   d) False: $\frac{3}{12} = \frac{1}{4}$

5. False: $\frac{3}{8}$, $\frac{7}{12}$ and $\frac{15}{20}$ are not equivalent to $\frac{1}{2}$

Explain how you know
Pupils' reasoning will vary. You will need to review individual explanations and make sure they are valid.
1. No. There are 12 equal parts on the diagram. One-third of 12 = 4 so two-thirds of 12 = 4 × 2 = 8. Therefore, eight parts of the diagram should be shaded to show two-thirds.

2. Yes. The scale shows 1.3kg which is equivalent to 1300g so it is more than 1000g but less than 1500g.

3. I agree with Eddie because when you count in multiples of 1000 only the place value of the thousands column will change and the hundreds, tens and ones will always be zero.

4. No. I know this is not correct because if Su uses four times as much of the ingredients then she will make 24 cookies. To make 18 cookies, Su needs to use three times as much of the ingredients.

5. Yes, Amy is correct. A right-angled quadrilateral with an area of 18cm² would have a length of 6cm and a width of 3cm but, because the length and width are not equal, this shape is not a square but a rectangle.

Would you rather?
1. I would rather have £1000 more than £9089 which is equal to £10089 because this is greater than £1000 less than £10100 which is equal to £9100.
2. I would rather have 18 days' holiday as this is more than two weeks which is only equal to 14 days.
3. I would rather play on my computer for 12 minutes because this is equal to 720 seconds which is greater than 600 seconds.
4. I think Farmer Scott would rather have vegetable patch B as this gives him the greatest area (30m²) in which to grow his vegetables.
5. I would rather have £9.68 rounded to the nearest pound because I would get £10 whereas £9.49 rounded to the nearest pound is £9 so I would have £1 less.
6. I would rather have $\frac{1}{3}$ of £96 as this is equal to £32 which is more than $\frac{2}{5}$ of £65, which is £26.
7. I would rather give five sweets to Ravi as this is less than $\frac{3}{10}$ of 20, which is six sweets.

Odd one out
Pupils may have given different answers. Check that their answer and the reason they have given are valid.
1. c) because it is the only 2-D shape in the set that is not a quadrilateral or d) because it is the only shape in the set that does not have a right angle.
2. c) because it shows $\frac{3}{5}$ (= 0.6) and all the other fractions are equivalent to the decimal 0.4
3. c) because it is the only number that would be rounded down or b) as it is the only one that rounds to an odd number.
4. b) because it is equal to 40. The other answers are equal to 10.
5. b) because all the lengths are equal or d) because it is the only triangle with a right angle.

6. c) because it is the only one which is a whole number.

Always, sometimes, never true?

1. Always true: the value of the tenths tells us whether to round the ones up or down. If the value of the tenths is less than 5 then round down. If the value of the tenths is 5 or more then round up.

2. Never true: 1m = 100cm so 10m = 1000cm.

3. Sometimes true: 12-hour digital clocks use am and pm but 24-hour clocks and 12-hour analogue clocks do not.

4. Never true: the total sum of two right angles is 180 degrees and an acute angle is any angle less than 90 degrees.

5. Always true: the perimeter means the total distance around a shape.

6. Always true: $\frac{1}{5}$ is not equivalent to $\frac{2}{3}$, as this fraction bar shows:

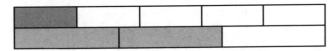

Convince me – What's the same? What's different?
Pupils may have given different answers. Check that their answer and the reason they have given are valid.

1. Same: the total value of each is 5315. Different: the number has been partitioned in different ways.

2. Same: they are all equivalent; they all represent part of a whole number. Different: two are fractions and one is a decimal representation.

3. Same: they are all quadrilaterals. Different: only the square and rectangles have four right angles.

4. Same: all the times show the equivalent of seven days. Different: time presented in different ways.

5. Same: all show data about the number of birds visiting a garden; all show that there were four blackbirds, two sparrows, six robins, two blue tits and eight other types of bird. Different: different types of chart.

If the answer is X, what is the question?
These are just suggestions. There are many possible correct answers.

1. 1500 + 500
5000 – 3000
Double 1000
Half of 4000
Quarter of 8000
500 × 4

2. If 1kg of potatoes costs £2 and 1kg of carrots costs £1.25, what is the cost of 4kg of potatoes and 2kg of carrots? A jacket costing £21 is in a 'half-price' sale. What is the new price?

3. Convert 6.5km to metres. A train travels $3\frac{1}{4}$ km from London to Burheade. How far does the train travel on a return journey from London to Burheade? Which is the greater distance: 6500m or 6km?

4. I am a multiple of 6 and 3 and less than 20. My ones digit is an even number and the sum of my digits is one less than 10. Deepa builds a six-brick tower. Zoe's tower is three times taller. How many bricks tall is Zoe's tower?

5. Dan catches the 4:55pm bus and takes a 45-minute journey home. What time does he get home?

6. What is $\frac{2}{3}$ subtracted from one whole?

7. What is the value of the digit 5 in the number 36.58?

8. What is $\frac{1}{5}$ of 10kg?

Answers: Topic-by-topic pupil activities

Note: Answers will often vary. Some sample answers are provided for guidance. Teachers should use their judgment when reviewing pupils' responses to open-ended questions and when assessing their reasoning.

Number sequences

1. a) Rule: +6 (24, 30, 36, 42, 48)
    b) Rule: +25 (100, 125, 150, 175, 200)
    c) Rule: +7 (28, 35, 42, 49, 56)
    d) Rule: +1000 (5000, 6000, 7000, 8000, 9000)
    e) Rule: −25 (50, 25, 0, −25, −50)
    f) Rule: −9 (−27, −36, −45, −54, −63)

2. a) False: 50 more tickets were sold on Day 1 than on Day 2.
    b) True
    c) False: there was a decrease of 25 tickets.
    d) True

3. Always true: an odd number added to an odd number is an even number and an odd number added to an even number is an odd number. This happens alternately in the seven times table.

4. No, I disagree because the 5th pattern will look like this, so there will be nine triangles and six squares.

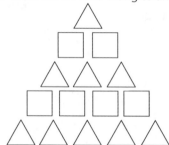

5. Same: both count in constant step sizes. There are multiples of 3 on both squares. Different: square 1 counts in 6s, square 2 counts in 9s, negative numbers are included on square 1, square 1 is a 4 × 4 grid; square 2 is a 4 × 3 grid.

6. a) For example: 6, 12, 18, 24, 30, 36, …
    b) For example: 1, 7, 13, 19, 25, 31, 37, …
    c) For example: −15, −9, −3, 3, 9, 15, 21, 27, …

Number and place value

1. True: the largest possible 4-digit number is 9999 which has 9 thousands.

2. a) I agree with Amy – the number Raj has made is 4307
    b) Yes, the number will be 5306 which is greater than 5000

3. a) £1000 more than £3888
    b) £1000 less than £3004
    c) £1000 more than £192

4. Sam is correct that XXIV (24) is the smallest number missing from the Roman numeral 100 grid. However, Jon is incorrect because the largest number missing is 77 which is written as LXXVII.

5. B, C and E

6. For example: 8 thousands, 6 hundreds, 7 tens and 0 ones
    8 thousands, 6 hundreds, 70 ones
    86 hundreds, 7 tens and 0 ones
    867 tens and 0 ones

7. Same: same value of hundreds and tens in each number; all numbers round down when rounding to the nearest 10; all numbers round up when rounding to the nearest 100 or nearest 1000. Different: value of the thousands digit and the ones digit.

Addition

1. a) True
    b) True
    c) True
    d) False: 6894 + 3201 = 10 095
        One has not been carried over from the hundreds to the thousands column.
    e) True

2. 3962 miles (1264 + 1264 + 1434)

3. Yes, I agree with Belle because the largest 4-digit number possible is 9999: 9999 + 9999 = 19 998
    Therefore, the total is less than one million.

4. For example: 3000 + 2250, 3470 + 1780, 2650 + 2600, 1985 + 3265

5. Su: 4379, Amy: 7147

6. For example: 2760 + 4315, 2651 + 4073

7.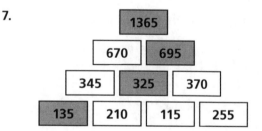

Subtraction

1. £1900

2. a) Incorrect: has not exchanged tens to take away ones.

$$\begin{array}{r} 6 \,\, {}^{4}\!\!\not{5} \,\, {}^{18}\!\!\not{8} \,\, {}^{1}1 \\ -\,3 \,\, 2 \,\, 9 \,\, 8 \\ \hline 3 \,\, 2 \,\, 9 \,\, 3 \end{array}$$

    b) Correct

c) Incorrect: tens column should be 14 − 5 = 9 rather than 8

```
      7  1
   3  8  4  9
−  2  7  5  8
   1  0  9  1
```

d) Incorrect: 2 − 2 = 0 rather than 4

```
   5  1
   8  3  4  2
−  3  7  1  2
   2  6  3  0
```

3. c) as it is the only one that involves exchanging.

4. I disagree because you get to 3030 after four subtractions of 1205 from 7850

5. Ben: 6777, Jack: 3251

6. Check pupils' calculations are correct and that they have described a suitable strategy.
9999 − 1237 is the largest possible answer.
9999 − 9973 is the smallest possible answer.

7. Sometimes true: for example, you would exchange a hundred to complete these calculations

```
  3437          or          4465
−2162                      −2193
```

but you would **not** exchange a hundred to complete:

```
  4688          or          3768
−3164                      −1954
```

Addition and subtraction

1. I disagree with both Ali and Tara because:
7632 − 5489 = 2143
1889 + 996 = 2885
so you need to use the symbol < between the calculations.

2. For example: 3000 + 1596; 2340 + 2256; 5852 − 1256; 6641 − 2045

3. **a)** The inverse calculation is incorrect as Jay has not exchanged a ten when subtracting the ones.
b) Correct

4. **a)** 2775 = 1706 + 1069
2775 − 1706 = 1069
2775 − 1069 = 1706
b) 3854 + 5321 = 9175
9175 − 3854 = 5321
9175 − 5321 = 3854
c) 6698 = 3819 + 2879
6698 − 3819 = 2879
6698 − 2879 = 3819

5.

1352	3718	2028
3042	2366	1690
2704	1014	3380

Magic number = 7098

6.

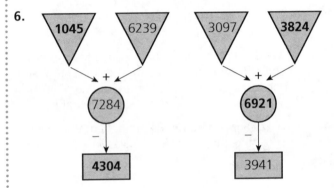

Multiplication

1. **a)** True
b) False: 58 × 9 = 50 × 9 + 8 × 9 or 60 × 9 − 2 × 9
c) False: 24 × 6 = 10 × 6 + 10 × 6 + 4 × 6 or 20 × 6 + 4 × 6
d) True

2.

×	7	12
9	63	108
4	28	48
8	56	96

3. 589 × 6 = 3534 tins

4. I disagree: 100 × 6 − 1 × 6 would be the same as 99 × 6. Therefore, to calculate 98 × 6 you would need to do 100 × 6 − 2 × 6

5. Same: answer is 1060; operation is multiplication. Different: first method is short multiplication and second method is expanded multiplication using place value counters to make arrays.

6. For example: 978 × 4 = 3912, 487 × 9 = 4383, 874 × 9 = 7866 (largest product)

7. 9 times table: J = 9, D = 1, B = 3, E = 2, A = 7, C = 8, K = 4, F = 6, H = 5

Division

1. b) because it is the only division calculation with a remainder.

Answers: Topic-by-topic pupil activities

2. Group A because I would receive the greatest amount of winnings: 189 ÷ 3 = £63
Group B = 275 ÷ 5 = £55
Group C = £288 ÷ 9 = £32
Group D = £266 ÷ 7 = £38

3. Yes, I agree because 495 ÷ 9 = 55

4. **a)** 69
b) 89
c) 58

5. d) because you would need to use the calculation 378 × 7

6. Leyla has calculated 68 × 7 = 476 and then incorrectly calculated 68 × 4 = 272 and added 476 + 272 to make 748 seeds. She should have calculated 68 × 7 = 476 and then added the four seeds that were left over so 476 + 4 = 480 seeds.

7. Any multiple of 9 + 3; any multiple of 9 + 5

Multiplication and division
1. **a)** 189 bricks
b) 66 times smaller
c) 34m

2. 16 combinations

3.
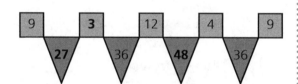

4. ● = 9; ▲ = 8; ★ = 12
Missing column total = 57; missing row total = 63

5. 70cm and 42cm

6. **a)** False: 84 sweets ÷ 4 = 21; Ricky has 21 × 3 = 63 sweets; Charlie has 21 × 1 = 21 sweets
b) True

Fractions 1
1. **a)** True
b) False: $\frac{11}{9}$
c) True
d) False: $\frac{3}{7}$

2. Same: all divided into six equal parts, each part represents $\frac{1}{6}$ of the whole. Different: each part of the hexagon is the same, so shape and area are congruent; the shapes in the rectangle are different but each has the same quantity.

3. I disagree because the lengths of the two strips are not the same. $\frac{2}{4} = \frac{4}{8}$

4. **a)** $\frac{3}{8}$ of £256 = £96 which is greater than $\frac{2}{3}$ of £102 = 68
b) $\frac{9}{12}$ of £144 = £108 which is greater than $\frac{7}{9}$ of £126 = £98
c) $\frac{4}{6}$ of £324 = £216 which is greater than $\frac{2}{7}$ of £392 = £112

5. Any six rectangles shaded in different combinations. 19 possible combinations in total.

6. For example: $\frac{5}{8} + \frac{9}{8} + \frac{2}{8}$ or $\frac{6}{8} + \frac{6}{8} + \frac{4}{8}$ or $\frac{3}{8} + \frac{7}{8} + \frac{6}{8}$

7. E = 1, O = 0, A = 5, F = 2, D = 6, G = 3

Fractions 2
1.
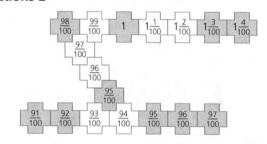

2. I disagree because 5.9 and 6.6 rounded to the nearest whole numbers are 6 and 7 so an approximate answer is 6 + 7 = 13

3. 6 ÷ 100 is equivalent to $\frac{6}{100}$ so it is the odd one out as the others are all fraction and decimal representations showing $\frac{6}{10}$

4. **a)** For example: 7.82 > 6.34, 6.87 > 4.32, 8.67 > 2.43
b) For example: 4.67 < 8.32, 7.23 < 8.64, 4.83 < 7.26

5. **a)** Sometimes true: e.g. 6.1 < 8.3 but 36.1 < 28.3
b) Never true
c) Sometimes true: e.g. 6.21 > 6.12 but 6.21 < 6.42

6. 12, 18, 30, 36, 54, 60, 72, 78

7. 0.25, 0.7, 0.05, 0.4

Measures 1
1. **a)** True
b) False: 7.5 litres = 7500mL which is greater than 7050mL.
c) False: 400g is less than 0.5 kg which is 500g.
d) True
e) True
f) False: 6546mL is greater than 6.5 litres which is 6500mL.

2. 300g

3. $\frac{3}{4}$ of 3 litres is 2250mL which is the greatest amount.

4. 225.5km

5. 0.675 litres

6. For example: 2 × bowl + 2 × bottle + 14 × jugs

7. First jug: 3 litres. Second jug: 3 × 1.5 = 4.5 litres. Third jug: 4.5 × 1.5 = 6.75 litres, so the third jug holds 6.75 litres not 9 litres.

8. For example:

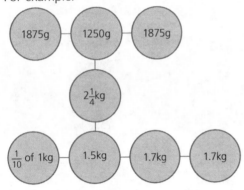

Measures 2

1. Shape C has an area of 30cm² whereas Shape A and Shape B are both 24cm²

2. 19.22m

3. Two short sides = 18 × 2 = 36cm
Total perimeter 102cm – 36cm = 66cm
Liv has forgotten to divide 66cm by 2 to find the length of each long side. So 66 ÷ 2 = 33cm.

4. He should rent allotment A as it is 7 × 12 = 84m² and allotment B is only 9 × 7 = 63m² so A gives him an extra 21m² of space.

5. Sometimes true. If the length of the rectangle is longer than the side of the square but the width is shorter, it is only sometimes the case that the perimeter is longer. For example:

6. For example:

7. Yes, she is correct because the × fact for 63cm² is 9 × 7 which would mean the length and the width of the shape would be different so it cannot be a square. 63 is not a square number.

8. Each tile is 2m long and 0.5m wide.
The centre square has a length of 2m – 0.5m = 1.5m.
The perimeter of the square is 4 × 1.5 = 6m.

Money

1.
a) True
b) False: £6.99 is greater than £6.89 because there are 9 tenths in £6.99 and only 8 tenths in £6.89
c) False: £7.98 is greater than £7.69 because there are 9 tenths in £7.98 and only 6 tenths in £7.69
d) False: £3.75 + £1.25 = £5.00 which is greater than £4.50
e) True

2. 80p saving

3. I agree with Oscar.
Beth paid 65p per can (£2.60 ÷ 4 = 65p)
Oscar paid 48p per can (£2.88 ÷ 6 = 48p)

4.
a) 2:20pm
b) £6.25 (assuming it is possible to hire for $\frac{1}{2}$ hour, otherwise £7.50)

5.

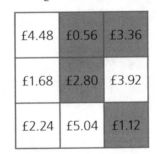

Magic number = £8.40

6. A = £3, B = £5, C = £7

7. He is incorrect because the total money is £2.60 ÷ 4 = 65p; 65p × 3 = £1.95
So Sid needs to take £1.95 in coins: £1 coin, 50p coin, 2 × 20p coins and 1 × 5p coin.

8. Set 1 = £7.95; $\frac{2}{3}$ of £7.95 = £2.65 × 2 = £5.30
Set 2 = £8.70; $\frac{2}{3}$ of £8.70 = £2.90 × 2 = £5.80, so this would be more money.

Time

1. Sometimes true. If both consecutive years have 365 days then the total number of days will be 730. However, if one year is a leap year (366 days), then there will be 731 days.

Answers: Topic-by-topic pupil activities

2. **Set 1** c) as it shows a morning time.

Set 2 d) as it shows an evening time.

3. 380 minutes = 6 hours 20 minutes

4. I agree with Bes. Noah ran the race in 312 seconds (5 minutes 12 seconds) which is 7 seconds slower than Bes's time of 5 minutes 5 seconds.

5. Same: they all show 7:35. Different: they all show the time in different ways, e.g. digital, analogue, some show pm, others do not.

6.
a) True: castle tour is 30 minutes while the museum tour is 45 minutes.
b) False: 420 seconds.
c) False: $\frac{1}{3}$ of 6 hours = 2 hours but the tour of the cathedral is 2 hours 10 minutes.
d) False: the tours add to 3 hours 32 minutes.

7.
a) I would rather have $\frac{1}{6}$ of 4 hours which is 40 minutes so I get 5 minutes extra.
b) I would rather have $\frac{1}{10}$ of 65 minutes which is 390 seconds which is longer than 300 seconds.

8. Any start time between 14:15 and 14:50 with corresponding finish time

Properties of shapes
1. Same: they are all 2-D shapes, all quadrilaterals, all have four sides, all are polygons. Different: they do not all have right angles or perpendicular lines or symmetry.

2.
a) Always true
b) Sometimes true: a right-angled triangle can be an isosceles where the two other equal angles are 45°.
c) Never true: a scalene triangle has three different lengths and three different size angles.
d) Always true

3. Wadha is incorrect as angles B and D are greater than 90° so are obtuse angles.

4. Ruby's shape: square
Tom's shape: trapezium
Sam's shape: rhombus

5.
a) Accept a range of different triangles that have been labelled correctly.
b) Accept a range of different quadrilaterals that have been labelled correctly.

6. No, I don't agree. The crosses need to be in the squares shown below.

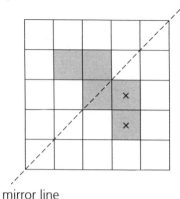

mirror line

7. The number of lines of symmetry is equivalent to the number of sides of a regular polygon.

Position and direction
1.
a) False: state the x-coordinate first, so it should be (3, 5).
b) True
c) False: it should be (2, 2).

2. Same: the x of the coordinate is the same for A and C and also for B and D because the points are at the same distance from the y-axis. The y of the coordinate is the same for A and B and also for D and C because the points are at the same height from the x-axis. Different: the x coordinates between A and B, and A and D; the x coordinates between C and B, and C and D; the y coordinates between A and C, and A and D; the y coordinates between B and C, and B and D.

3. I disagree. The coordinate for point C should be (5, 2) in order for all points to be joined to make a rectangle.

4. I agree. Point A moves 3 squares to the right and 3 squares up.

5. Answers will vary according to the shape and rule chosen.

Statistics
1.
a) False: each lollipop symbol represents 9 so there are 18 strawberry lollipops.
b) True
c) False: there are 45 sunshine yellow lollipops and 9 iceflake lollipops so there are 36 fewer iceflake lollipops.
d) False: there are 11 lollipop symbols in total on the pictogram so 11 × 9 = 99 lollipops in total.

2. Lexi is incorrect because the chart shows that the children went walking 227 times over the months of May, June and July but only went sailing 109 times.

3. **a)** 75 pupils
    b) 25 pupils
    c) Bicycle and tram
    d) 175 pupils

4. Jenna is incorrect because the depth of the bath remained the same from 9 minutes to 17 minutes which is 8 minutes.

End-of-year test

1. 85 hundreds, 4 tens and 2 ones
    854 tens and 2 ones
    8 thousands, 54 hundreds and 2 ones
    8 thousands, 5 hundreds, 42 ones

2. Darius: 5287, Jelena: 1861

3. Sometimes true. In the calculation 3487 – 2341, you would not need to exchange a hundred. However, in the calculation 3487 – 2391 or 5321 – 7280, you would need to exchange a hundred to complete the calculation.

4. 51 times

5. I disagree because the lengths of the two strips are not the same. $\frac{1}{2}$ is equal to $\frac{4}{8}$ not $\frac{3}{8}$

6. I would rather have $\frac{4}{9}$ of £324 because I would receive £144. This is larger than $\frac{2}{3}$ of £189 which is equal to £126

7. **a)** For example: 2678 is the odd one out because it is the only number which does not have 4 tens.
    b) For example: 291 is the odd one out because it is the only number which has 2 hundreds/only number with 3 digits; the others have 2 thousands/4 digits.

8. Same: the tally chart, bar chart and table show the same number of roses, daisies, pansies and other flowers; all are charts that show data in a clear way. Different: the bar chart shows seven tulips while the table and tally chart show four tulips; different types of chart.

9. For example: $\frac{3}{10} + \frac{2}{10} + \frac{5}{10}$

10. 40 matchsticks

11. Same: all polygons, all quadrilaterals, all have at least one set of parallel lines. Different: not all shapes have a pair of perpendicular lines, one shape only has one set of parallel lines, one shape doesn't have any right angles.

12.

160	580	280
460	340	220
400	100	520

Magic number = 1020

13. I would rather have £1000 more than £1101 because it is £1100 more than the other option.

14. For example: 1000 + 4250; 2500 + 2750; 5000 + 250; 2625 + 2625

15. For example: 4.83 < 9.61; 3.91 < 4.68; 1.49 < 6.83

16. b) because it has an area of 25cm² while the other two shapes both have an area of 18cm²

17. Zoe is correct because a shape with an area of 27cm² would have a length of 9cm and a width of 3cm. The length and width are not equal, so this shape is not a square.

18. I agree with Osma because he paid 75p per can whereas Tia has paid £1.25 per can.

19. 17:15

20. Twenty-five to eight in the evening is the odd one out as it should say twenty-five to nine in the evening to match all the other times.

21. Yes, I agree because 32 seeds × 6 pots = 192 seeds and 192 seeds + 4 seeds left over = 196 seeds.

22. 4095 – 2535 = 1560; 4095 – 1560 = 2535; 1560 + 2535 = 4095

23. I agree with Tara because 3904 – 672 = 3232 and 1889 + 299 = 2188. Therefore 3904 – 672 is greater than (>) 1889 + 299

24. Always true

25. **a)** Rule: add 6 (24, 30, 36, 42, 48)
    b) Rule: add 25 (100, 125, 150, 175, 200)

26. **a)** False: in an equilateral triangle all the angles are the same size.
    b) False: an isosceles triangle has two sides of equal length.
    c) True

27. I disagree because 85 multiplied by 8 = 680 and Mrs Chen needs 685 pencils. Mrs Chen needs to buy 86 packs so she has enough pencils for all the pupils.

28. B, D, E

29. b) because it is a right angle while all the other angles are obtuse.

30. Triangle: 25; star: 6; circle: 1000

Year 4 problem solving and reasoning pupil target sheet

Finding all possibilities	Achieved ✓	Achieved ✓	Achieved ✓
I respond to and ask questions such as 'What can we try next?' or 'What if …?' to help solve the problem.			
I am beginning to develop systematic ways for finding **all** solutions, e.g. looking at one shape at a time or starting with the smallest number.			
I am beginning to know the best method to record all possible solutions, e.g. an ordered list.			
I can find and prove that I have found all possible answers to a problem.			
Finding rules and describing patterns			
I can independently describe the rule of a sequence involving numbers or shapes.			
I can test if the rule works for other predicted terms in the sequence.			
I can independently continue the sequence.			
I can independently use the found rule to work out the tenth term in a sequence.			
Logic puzzles			
I can independently recognise some patterns and relationships in the information given.			
I can independently use the given facts and put them in order of importance to help solve the problem, e.g. looking for where there is only one unknown.			
I can independently explore what happens if I only use one piece of information and can begin to explain what effect it has.			
I respond to 'What if …?' questions and recognise the effect.			
I can independently use the information given to help find missing facts to solve the problem.			
I can independently check and explain that the solution meets all of the criteria.			
Real-life word problems			
I can solve problems involving money using decimal notation £.p.			
I can solve problems involving time.			
I can solve simple problems that involve converting between units of measure.			
I can solve problems involving integer scaling, e.g. the shopping trolley is 12 times heavier than the shopping basket.			
I can measure and calculate the perimeter of rectilinear shapes.			
I can find the area of rectilinear shapes by counting squares.			
Reasoning			
I can identify if a statement is true or false; always, sometimes or never true and recognise the odd one out.			
I can explain what's the same and what's different.			
I am beginning to explain my reasoning using clear sentence structures, calculations and diagrams.			
I can give at least one other example to back up my reasoning.			